The Roots of
Anti-
Semitism

HEIKO A. OBERMAN

The Roots of
Anti-
Semitism

In the Age of Renaissance and Reformation

translated by
James I. Porter

FORTRESS PRESS   PHILADELPHIA

Translated by James I. Porter from the German *Wurzeln des Antisemitismus* © 1981 by Severin und Siedler, Berlin, Federal Republic of Germany.

English translation copyright © 1984 by Fortress Press

Library of Congress Cataloging in Publication Data.

Oberman, Heiko Augustinus.
  The roots of anti-Semitism in the age of Renaissance and Reformation.

  Translated by James I. Porter from the German, Wurzeln des Antisemitismus—T.p. verso.
  Includes bibliographical references.
  1. Christianity and antisemitism—History—16th century. 2. Reformation. 3. Martin, Luther, 1843–1546—Attitude toward Judaism. 4. Judaism. I. Title.
II. Title: Roots of antisemitism in the age of Renaissance and Reformation.
BM535.02413 1983   261.2'6   83–5695
ISBN 0–8006–0709–0

K122D83 Printed in the United States of America 1–709

Dedicated to
RABBI MARTIN E. KATZENSTEIN
1922–70

*"determined to bear
this division in common"*

Contents

Preface

The immediate occasion for this book was an invitation to contribute to a Festschrift in honor of Martin Luther's five-hundredth birthday, 10 November 1983. From the many challenging possibilities that came to mind, I immediately decided upon the topic of "Luther and the Jews," convinced that in the round of festivities, reflection on this sensitive aspect of the life and thought of the reformer should not be neglected.

Such a decision, of course, is long in the making and actually much less spontaneous than one might like to admit. Born and raised in the Netherlands, I can trace my earliest impressions back to 10 May 1940, the date of the German invasion of my country and the key experience of my youth. I virtually grew up with the topic "Germany and the Jews." Interest in this matter accompanied me to Oxford where I engaged in research ten years after the victory of the Allies. There, in the lecture halls and in the clubs, I encountered an anti-Semitism couched in humor, but nonetheless brazen—something which was unthinkable in Holland and which would be most egregious in Germany today. The romantic ideal I had formed of Britain during the dark years of the occupation, when this birthplace of parliamentary government had become the very symbol of victory and freedom, was sobered by this encounter. Clearly, the matter could not be restricted to Germany; my reflection on it had to be broadened to include "Europe and the Jews."

My next journey abroad involved an eight-year stay in the United States while teaching at Harvard University. There I confronted a diverse and vital Jewish culture, both at the university among professors and away from the campus among an educated, historically aware, and active "laity." I recall with gratitude the joyful and warmhearted wisdom of Rabbi Martin Katzenstein (d. 1970), who introduced me to the Judaic delight in creation and law. This book is dedicated to him.

At the time the air was thick with news reports on the lengthy and agonizing trial of Adolf Eichmann in Jerusalem. In this tension-packed climate, a tough discussion was underway within Rabbi Katzenstein's congregation between recent immigrants who had escaped the liquidation camps and American-born Jews. To the former, questions of guilt and revenge were as pressing as life itself, while to the latter those obsessions represented a hate-engendering slavery to the past. As a representative of a country that had "suffered at the hands of the Germans on non-racial grounds," I was invited to a panel discussion on the topic of "The Germans and the Jews." I had imagined that I was in complete accord with the audience until I found myself being told by a survivor of Auschwitz, "You Christians are to blame for everything, with your centuries of Jew-baiting." I was thus abruptly ejected from the circle of victims, only to be drawn further into a confrontation with the age-old historical question of the relationship between Christians and Jews.

This question could not but become all the more acute as I moved from Harvard to Tübingen. In my fifteen years as a resident observer I have discovered—though at first reluctantly—that the history of the Third Reich is both intensively and unsparingly pursued in the press and on television, in the lecture hall and in the family circle, and even by non-Christians in the spirit of the 19 October 1945 Stuttgart confession of the Protestant churches. Moreover, on 11 January 1980, the national convention of the evangelical church placed on its agenda theses leading "Toward a renewal of the relationship between Christians and Jews," the discussion of which had broad repercussions beyond the boundaries of the church. The questions of guilt and complicity were there so thoroughly aired that the faculty of evangelical theology at the university in Bonn felt compelled to reply: "The national socialist ideology was just as openly unchristian and anti-Christian as it was anti-Jewish." "Just as openly . . ." Historians in Germany and exiled Germans alike were stunned. Was this a German apology?

Circumstances have obliged me to put aside the experiences of my travels and to restrict the discussion of such a calamitous history once again to "Germany and the Jews." In a public statement delivered on 19 June 1981, the Israeli prime minister, Menachem Begin, was able to document the historic, collective guilt of the Germans with a citation from Luther's late works without drawing a contradiction from any source. But the image of Luther on which

Begin based his remarks is by no means a typically Israeli construc-
tion; it had been previously sketched in its essentials by several
renowned German Luther scholars. Even the present book was, as
already mentioned, originally conceived as an investigation of
"Luther and the Jews," though the progress of the work has made it
necessary to expand the topic to the Jewish question in the sixteenth
century, the transition from the Middle Ages to the early modern era.

Owing to the historical relevance and the contemporary explo-
siveness of the subject, some footnotes have proven indispensable,
although three scholarly articles which I have published elsewhere
make an exhaustive documentation available, and reference to these
is provided below.

The title calls for two remarks. Strictly speaking, "anti-Semitism"
did not exist prior to the race theory of the nineteenth century.
Nevertheless, there are events, attitudes, or statements which long
before the rise of the concept come very close to the reality of
anti-Semitism. More problematic still is the part of the title that
concerns the "roots" of anti-Semitism, since these admittedly reach
further back than the sixteenth century. The search for roots conceals the danger of wishing to absolve Christianity entirely in every
period. St. Augustine (d. 430), for example, could already cite a
pagan, the Roman philosopher Seneca (d. 65), as his authority for the
fact that the Jews were "an arch-criminal race" *(sceleratissima gens)*.

And yet hatred of the Jews was not an invention of the sixteenth
century. It was an inherited assumption. Far from acquitting the age
of Renaissance and Reformation, we should recognize that this same
age which so consciously scrutinized the medieval traditions simultaneously passed on, with new strength, whatever withstood the test
of inspection. This is what stamps the character of the age and
determines its significance for the modern era.

This book could not have been written without the resources of the
British Museum, without the undisturbed quiet of Ekeby, or without
constant dialogue with Manfred Schulze. He not only reworked the
list of the *dramatis personae,* but himself became an active agent as a
colleague in the search for the connection between past and present.

Tübingen   Heiko A. Oberman
15 September 1981

When the Lord restored the fortunes of Zion,
  we were like those who dream.
Then our mouth was filled with laughter,
  and our tongue with shouts of joy;
then they said among the nations,
  "The Lord has done great things for them."
The Lord has done great things for us;
  we are glad.
Restore our fortunes, O Lord,
  like the watercourses in the Negeb!
May those who sow in tears
  reap with shouts of joy!
He that goes forth weeping,
  bearing the seed for sowing,
shall come home with shouts of joy,
  bringing his sheaves with him.

Psalm 126 (RSV)

Dramatis Personae

In what follows, those figures who took an active part in the history that is about to be related here are presented by way of introduction, in alphabetical order.

1. Martin Bucer
2. John Calvin
3. Wolfgang Capito
4. Duke Eberhard the Bearded
5. Johannes Eberlin of Günzburg
6. Johannes Eck
7. Erasmus of Rotterdam
8. Elector Frederick the Wise
9. Jakob von Hochstraten
10. Balthasar Hubmaier
11. Ulrich von Hutten
12. Justus Jonas
13. Josel of Rosheim
14. Martin Luther
15. Philipp Melanchthon
16. Andreas Osiander
17. Johannes Pfefferkorn
18. Johannes Reuchlin
19. Huldreich Zwingli

1. Martin Bucer (1491–1551)

Bucer was born in Schlettstadt (Sélestat) in Alsace, in whose renowned Latin school he was introduced to humanistic ideals. He was forced to break off his pursuit of the liberal arts when at age fifteen he entered the Dominican order. While studying at Heidelberg, he encountered Luther for the first time at a large public disputation held by the Augustinians (April 1518) and was directly won over to the cause of the Reformation. Released from his vows with papal permission and now a secular priest, Bucer became one of the first reformers to marry (1522). Over the next quarter-century, from the time of his appointment as a pastor in a suburb of Strasbourg (1524) until his forced emigration to Cambridge during the Interim (1548), Bucer promoted and defended the Reformation in Strasbourg.

His influence extended far beyond Alsace, and he used his position in efforts to mediate between Wittenberg and Zurich. The appointment of Calvin to a pastorate in Strasbourg strengthened Bucer's influence with Reformed Protestantism. In the last years of his life in exile in England, he took part in the editing of the *Book of Common Prayer,* thus leaving his mark on the cornerstone of the Anglican church as well.

2. John Calvin (1509–1564)

The French exile stepped into the forefront of the Reformation's second generation as a young man, chiefly through the publication of his *Institutes of the Christian Religion* (1st ed., Basel, 1536). Calvin's high regard for Luther led him to reevaluate the latter's theological discoveries, and the independent interpretation Calvin developed gave his "mother church" in Geneva and the whole of European Protestantism a new flavor, one that was more independent of secular rulers than the Wittenberg model.

In the course of his legal studies in Orléans and Bourges (1527–29), Calvin encountered the French strain of humanism, a movement that was led especially by jurists who had cultivated a taste for the effectiveness of eloquence and a thirst after the origins of Roman law. He then moved to Paris to sharpen his proficiency in the classical languages at the newly established Collège Royal. But it was only later, once he had immersed himself in Hebrew while in exile at Basel and Strasbourg, that he became *trilinguis,* that is, truly trilingual. In his first independent publication, a commentary on Seneca's *De clementia* (1532), he ventured to supplement and revise editions of Seneca by Erasmus (1515, 1529).

His decision to join the Reformation (1533/34) forced him to forego the scholarly life of which he had dreamt. His understanding of questions of law and his knowledge of the patristic authorities (a knowledge equaled only by Erasmus and Melanchthon) were now placed in the service of building up the churches of Geneva (1536–38; 1541–46) and Strasbourg (1538–41). Beyond this, Calvin's concern was to minister to the widely dispersed Protestant congregations which suffered persecution "under the cross of affliction"; his attentions were turned first toward France and soon after to Italy, Poland, the Netherlands, and Scotland.

Calvin's insistence on the distinctness of church and state and his efforts to keep doctrine and Christian discipline free from the interference of the secular authorities did not endear him to most oligarchical, urban regimes. Wherever Calvinism did gain a political foothold, it showed itself capable of a stifling intolerance; and yet, by this same means, the congregations of the diaspora became habituated to a characteristic independence in matters of church discipline and articles of faith.

3. Wolfgang Capito (1478–1541)

A doctor of theology (Freiburg, 1515), the Alsatian-born Capito was eminently qualified both for the position of pastor at the cathedral in Basel and for teaching responsibilities at the university there. Against the wishes and example of his teacher, Erasmus, he plunged into an intensive study of the Hebrew language and, together with Konrad Pellikan and Sebastian Münster, produced a complete Hebrew edition of the Psalms, the first of its kind to appear in a German-speaking land (November 1516). Earlier, in 1512, Reuchlin had issued an edition of the seven penitential psalms. Two years after his full edition of the Psalms, Capito once more drew upon the work of Reuchlin, this time his *Rudimenta,* and supplemented it with a companion manual—a grammar in two volumes (1518).

After reading and publishing texts of Luther in the fall of 1518, Capito discovered support for Luther's central ideas in his own biblical exegesis, with the result that the former Erasmian and steadfast Reuchlinist now aligned himself with Luther.

As one of the reformers of Strasbourg and a colleague of Martin Bucer, he provided Josel of Rosheim with a letter of introduction to Luther (1537), when the Jews in electoral Saxony were faced with the threat of expulsion.

4. Duke Eberhard the Bearded of Württemberg (1445–96)

A man of conscious purpose, Count Eberhard undertook to reunite the landgraviate of Württemberg, which had been divided since 1442. The Treaty of Münsinger (1482) brought about the reunion of his own Uracher line with that of Stuttgart. Emperor Maximilian was thus indebted to Eberhard and promoted him to the rank of Duke of Württemberg and Teck (1495). Under the influence of such men as the learned Johannes Reuchlin and Johannes Vergenhans (1425–1510), the first rector of the University of Tübingen (which university Eberhard, as territorial sovereign, had founded in 1477), Eberhard evolved into a "Renaissance prince" and assumed responsibility for the intellectual and religious well-being of his land. For Eberhard this included, among other things, maintaining a "Jew-free" Württemberg, a provision which, according to his demand, was likewise written into the charter of the new territorial university.

Duke Eberhard's policy of territorial consolidation for Württemberg, within a region falling between Swiss and Hapsburg interests, was never secure. What progress Eberhard had made was placed in jeopardy by the headstrong conduct of his successor Duke Ulrich I (1487–1550) who, unscrupulous at the best of times, became in the aftermath of the peasant uprising led by "poor Conrad" (1514) a virtually unbridled force in the realm. After illegally seizing the imperial free city of Reutlingen (1519), Ulrich found himself in the summer of the same year outlawed by the newly elected emperor Charles V and, having alienated all support, was easily ousted from the Swabian League. But in 1534, supported by Hesse, France, and Strasbourg, he succeeded in regaining his duchy.

It took his son Christoph (d. 1568) to win back the trust of the Württemberg nobility. The task required, among other things, continuing Eberhard's Jewish policy. At the outset, Christoph was even prepared to have the Jews driven en masse from the whole of the empire (1550). In an agreement with Josel of Rosheim, however, it was finally resolved that the Jews would no longer be allowed to bypass the duke and appeal directly to the emperor in legal proceedings. In return, Christoph made the concession of supplying transit visas for Jews passing through his duchy; they remained barred, however, from residence there.

5. Johannes Eberlin of Günzburg (1468–1533)

Next to Luther, Eberlin was the most trenchant of the pamphleteers of the early Reformation. Eberlin began his career in the Franciscan order as lector in Tübingen (1519) after having taught in Basel and Freiburg. After relocating to Ulm, he broke with the order in 1521. Although well past his prime, according to the standards of his day, Eberlin then set out to write his chief work, *The Fifteen Confederates,* in which he laid out a comprehensive program of church and social reform that was steeped in the ideas of Luther. A series of important pamphlets followed, among them *The Bell Tower* (1522) and *A Loyal Warning,* both of which were aimed at moderating the rebellious peasants (1525). His last years were devoted to building up the evangelical church in Wertheim.

6. Johannes Eck (1486–1543)

Thanks to his studies at Heidelberg, Tübingen, Cologne, and Freiburg, this native Swabian was, at an early age, in a position to combine humanistic impulses with scholastic training. He has to be recognized as the most significant opponent of Luther and, more generally, of the entire Reformation. Because of his early involvement in the debate concerning indulgences and his determination to expose the Wittenberg reformer as a heretic during the Leipzig Disputation (1519), the learned professor of Ingolstadt contributed so significantly to the situation that the Luther "inquiry" quickly escalated into the Luther "affair." Eck prepared and expedited Luther's condemnation. The "refutation" of the 1530 Augsburg Confession is also chiefly Eck's work, and his contribution to the religious discussions of 1540–41, which represented the last attempt at reconciliation at the time, became a blueprint for Roman Catholic orthodoxy. The fundamental orientation of this orthodox position had already been mapped out *in extenso* in Eck's often reprinted and comprehensive work, his *Enchiridion* (1525).

7. Erasmus of Rotterdam (1496–1536)

Reared in the tradition of the fifteenth-century "modern devotion" *(devotio moderna),* educated in Deventer and Paris, and broadened by travel in Italy and England, Erasmus returned to the continent in the summer of 1514 already the "prince of the humanists." His fame stemmed primarily from his collection of classical aphorisms, *Adagia,* and from his satirical *Praise of Folly.* During a trip from Louvain to Basel he was stunned by the enthusiastic reception that greeted him: "Germany won me with its overwhelming display of adulation." In 1530, after he had retreated from Protestant Basel to the more predictably orthodox Freiburg, he could "pierce the illusion" of that enthusiasm: "It is a typically German response, when anybody dishes out any sort of crazy ideology, to snap it up immediately" (24 June 1530).

In his view, the reformers threatened peace, harmony, and the cause of "fine arts." True piety was thereby similarly endangered. On this account Erasmus had already in 1524 written against Luther in his *On Free Will.* His edition of the Greek New Testament (1516) became a textbook for reformers, but his program for reform and education was aimed at an entirely different, long-term amelioration of church and society; the means to this end was to be the humanizing effect of an upbringing rooted in the classical sources of wisdom. A renovated Europe meant for Erasmus, however, a Christian Europe free of Jews.

8. Elector Frederick the Wise (1463–1525)

Scion of the Ernestine line of the Wettin house, Frederick became electoral prince of Saxony in 1486 and founded his territorial university in Wittenberg in 1502. His extensive collection of relics, which he installed in the Castle Church of All Saints, made Wittenberg the ecclesiastical center of the electorate. As patron and protector of both university and church, Frederick was able to block Luther's summons to Rome and to arrange a hearing on German soil instead (Augsburg, 1518). After the reformer had been condemned by the pope, Frederick insisted—in opposition to all ecclesiastical prerogative—upon a second hearing, which took place before the Diet of Worms in 1521. At that time the unrepentant reformer was declared an outlaw by the emperor, and he subsequently found refuge in Frederick's castle, the Wartburg.

Upon Frederick's death midway through the Peasants' War (1524–26), the reins passed into the hands of his brother and co-regent, John the Steadfast (d. 1532). John proved to be an active intercessor on behalf of the Reformation, for instance, in his ecclesiastical visitation of electoral Saxony. His son, John Frederick the Magnanimous (1503–54), reared on the teachings of Luther, was captured in the Schmalkaldic War (1547) and lost his title and powers to his cousin, Duke Moritz of Saxony. In 1536 John Frederick had issued his Jewish mandate for Saxony, against which Josel of Rosheim sought to intervene by soliciting the aid of Luther.

9. Jakob von Hochstraten, O.P. (1460–1527)

After his activities as professor of theology in Louvain and prior of the Dominican monastery in Antwerp, Hochstraten was called to Cologne in 1504. Within a brief span he had acquired a fearful reputation as inquisitor of the ecclesiastical provinces of Cologne, Mainz, and Trier.

At the suggestion of the Jewish convert Pfefferkorn, Hochstraten demanded the immediate confiscation of Talmudic texts. His was also the guiding hand behind the proceedings against Reuchlin, which made Hochstraten the primary target of the satirical *Letters of Obscure Men* (1515, 1517). As a result of pressure from the leader of the free imperial knights, Franz von Sickingen, Hochstraten was deposed as prior in Cologne, though he could later claim as his personal victory Rome's condemnation of Reuchlin in the same year (1520).

Not long before, Hochstraten's fellow countryman, Daniel Bomberg of Antwerp (d. 1553), had successfully gained papal permission for the first printing of the complete Talmud (Venice, 1519–1523). On 12 August 1553, however, Pope Julius III nonetheless ordered the destruction of all Hebrew writings. In Venice, books were in flames even before the bonfires raged throughout the rest of the papal states.

10. Balthasar Hubmaier (1485–1528)

Hubmaier, the first "professional" theologian among the Anabaptists, received his academic training in Freiburg at the feet of Luther's future opponent, Johannes Eck. As cathedral pastor in Regensburg (1516–22), he turned vehemently against the Jewish community, which until then had stood under imperial protection. At Hubmaier's instigation, during the interregnum following the death of Emperor Maximilian (2 January 1519), the Jews were expelled within four days; their synagogue was leveled (21 February) and on its rubble the "Chapel of the Blessed Mary" was constructed.

As of the winter of 1522/23, Hubmaier numbered himself in the evangelical camp, and gained access to Zwingli in Zurich. His own "new" baptism in 1525, however, signaled a break with the Zurich reformer. Hubmaier was condemned and burned at the stake in Vienna (6 March 1528) for his conduct in Moravia, which had become a major center of Anabaptist activity.

11. Ulrich von Hutten (1488–1523)

This exceptionally gifted publicist early put his barbed quill at the service of Germany's liberation from Rome and the cause of intellectual reform through humanistic education. He joined Crotus Rubeanus to become a contributor to the second, more scathing volume of the *Letters of Obscure Men* published on behalf of Reuchlin. His motive was not, however, to protect the Jews but rather to combat the intellectual oppression instituted by Rome through its inquisitors and their professor in Cologne (Hochstraten) "who think with scholastic minds and allegedly speak Latin."

In the year 1517, Hutten received from Emperor Maximilian the highest distinction, being crowned poet laureate. After the unsuccessful revolt of the imperial knights under Franz von Sickingen (fall 1522), the already seriously ill Hutten sought safety at the side of Erasmus in Basel (end of 1522). Rejected by the timid humanist, Hutten directed his final polemical assault against his "betrayal" by the learned scholar whom he once revered as a courageous pioneer of freedom.

12. Justus Jonas (1493–1555)

During his student days at Erfurt, which culminated in the title of doctor of both laws, Roman and canonical (1518), Jonas revered Erasmus as "the mightiest king of learning." Erasmus personally encouraged him to study theology, and it was very likely through his friend the Erfurt Augustinian prior Johannes Lang that Jonas came into contact with Luther and eventually moved into the most intimate circle around the reformer in Wittenberg. He then became a constant companion to Luther. He was present in Worms at the Diet (1521); he celebrated Luther's marriage (1525); he took part in the Marburg Colloquy (1529); and finally, long recognized as a vigorous preacher, he delivered the sermon at Luther's grave.

With his immediate translation of Luther's polemical tract against Erasmus, *De servo arbitrio (On the Bondage of the Will)*, Jonas publicly documented his breach with his former idol and mentor, Erasmus. Jonas's humanistic proficiency in languages further put him in a position to make Luther accessible to the European world of letters by translating Luther's German writings into Latin. With regard to the Jewish question, however, we see how very much Luther's faithful companion and disciple nonetheless remained his own man.

13. Josel of Rosheim (1478–1554)

Three years after Josel managed to stave off the expulsion of the Jews from Oberehnheim in Alsace (1507), he was made *Parnos* and *Manhig*, "overseer" and "head," by the Alsatian Jewry. When Charles V (1519–55) was elected emperor, Josel succeeded in having the imperial privileges of the Jews reconfirmed at Charles's coronation ceremony in Aachen (1520). This was no small concern in view of the recent banishment of the Jews from Regensburg (1519).

The story of the tenacious exertions of this "ruler of German Jewry" reaches from his victorious disputation against the baptized Jew Antonius Margarita during the Diet of Augsburg in 1530, to the banning of Luther's tract *On the Jews and Their Lies* (1543) by the city council of Strasbourg, to a new promulgation of the imperial privileges of the Jews—the most comprehensive to date—at the Diet of Speyer (3 April 1544). The end result was, however, less spectacular. The privileges were pruned back by the imperial diet in February 1551.

14. Martin Luther (1483–1546)

When he posted his Ninety-five Theses (31 October 1517), this Augustinian monk and professor of theology at Wittenberg seemed at first merely to be renewing the medieval criticism of the commercialization of the church through the sale of indulgences. But Luther had explored the Scriptures so deeply, both in his monastic cell and in the lecture hall, that in his first public appearance he could compel the medieval church to reexamine the fundamental question—

buried under the abuses of the age—of fidelity to Scripture and latitude in faith.

Excommunicated in 1521 by the pope and outlawed by the emperor shortly thereafter in Worms, Luther was nonetheless able to pour his energies into the Reformation over the next quarter-century under the protection of his sovereigns, the electors of Saxony. With a barrage of crude, polemical pamphlets, carefully weighed expert opinions, lofty academic treatises, some three thousand often intensely personal letters, and—of great long-term effect—his original and highly inventive translations of the Old and New Testaments, Luther was the most popularly read man of his age.

After the Reformation movement had become associated with nonreligious or socially hazardous interests and had achieved definite political and social power, Luther consistently sought, to the end of his days—against princes, fellow citizens, peasants, and even against some within his own ranks—to define and defend the domain of Christian faith. In this definition, there was as little room for Jews as for popes and Turks.

15. Philipp Melanchthon (1497–1560)

Melanchthon became professor of Greek in Wittenberg upon the recommendation of his great-uncle, the Hebraist Reuchlin. In time he grew to be Luther's closest collaborator and trusted colleague. His inaugural lecture (29 May 1518) contained a comprehensive program of academic reforms based on classical literature, the fathers of the church, and the Scriptures. Up to this point Reuchlin and Erasmus could have found nothing to fault. But within the space of a year Melanchthon became a theologian in the spirit of Luther and, what is more, he openly displayed himself as Luther's disciple and ally through his participation in the Leipzig Disputation between Karlstadt, Luther, and Eck (1519). At this time he began to hold his own Bible lectures, out of which he developed his *Loci Communes* (1st ed., 1521), the first contribution to Protestant dogmatics, and a book which Luther praised throughout his life as the best synopsis of biblical theology.

Melanchthon's great powers of articulation made him a much-sought-after advisor and representative of electoral Saxony at diet sessions and at religious colloquies. He was the author of the first Lutheran confessional statement, the *Confessio Augustana,* a summary of the articles of faith as understood by Luther's adherents among the imperial estates. As the living embodiment of that fruitful blend of biblical humanism and Reformation theology, for which the

9

line between faith and erudition was as obvious as the difference between church and school, Melanchthon succeeded in transmitting the legacy of the Reformation, and in protecting it from the academic and cultural "no man's land" of a narrow-minded confessionalism.

16. Andreas Osiander (1498–1552)

Even during his first years of study at Ingolstadt (1515–?) Osiander very likely had already immersed himself in the study of the biblical languages. His primary models for Old and New Testament research were Reuchlin and Erasmus, and Reuchlin remained a lifelong inspiration. Appointed to the Augustinian monastery in Nuremberg as a Hebrew instructor in 1520, he came into daily contact with the "Martinians," those enthusiastic adherents of Luther who comprised a part of the humanistic circle that was pressing for reform. From then on he was regarded as a "Lutheran." Called to the church of St. Lorenz as a preacher, Osiander evolved into the reformer of Nuremberg. As such, he took part in the central events of the age: the Marburg Colloquy between Luther and Zwingli (1529), the Diet of Augsburg (1530), and the attempted unification between Eastern Orthodoxy and Protestantism at the ecumenical discussions in Hagenau and Worms (1540). Today one can no longer doubt his authorship of the anonymous preface to Nicholas Copernicus's major work, De revolutionibus orbium caelestium (1543). He had previously taken issue with the accusations against the Jews for ritual murders in another important and likewise anonymous document (1529).

When Emperor Charles V threatened to suppress the Reformation in the so-called Interim that followed his victory over the evangelical estates in 1548, Osiander had no choice but to withdraw from the empire to Königsberg. His final years (1549–52) were darkened by the schism that developed over the correct interpretation of Luther's teachings. When this conflict first came to a head, shortly before Osiander's death, Matthias Flacius, leader of the orthodox Lutherans, presented as evidence of Osiander's "unreliability" the fact that "eight years ago" (1543) he had written a letter to Luther which sharply criticized Luther's writings on the Jews.

This letter has not been preserved. Nevertheless it fits Osiander's profile exactly—to have "withstood" Luther "to the face" (Gal. 2:11) and to have censured the Wittenberg reformer for the harshness of his pronouncements on the Jews.

17. Johannes Pfefferkorn (d. ca. 1522)

Much about Pfefferkorn, including his birth and death dates, is uncertain. Even his conversion to the Christian faith and his resultant change of name from Joseph to Johannes (attested by the Council of Nuremberg on 10 September 1506) were, according to Pfefferkorn, affected one year earlier, and in Cologne.

In 1507, Pfefferkorn presented for the first time his proposal to confiscate and destroy all the Hebrew books of the Jews with the exception of the Bible, "since by these means they grow more firmly planted in their faithlessness." In the following years his writings appear, often in several places of publication at once and with ever-escalating aggression, demanding immediate missionary activity among the Jews and, finally, their expulsion. The Latin edition of his *Scourge of the Jews (Judenfeind,* 1509) is prefaced with a poem by the university professor and editor Ortwin Gratius (d. 1542); its theme is the "stiffnecked obstinacy" of the Jews. Pfefferkorn stood from this time onward under the protection of the university of Cologne and the Dominican order. But as soon as the *Letters of Obscure Men* (1515, 1517) absorbed public attention with its caricature of Pfefferkorn's protective patrons in Cologne, ridiculing them as ignorant robe-racks whose Latin was deplorable, Pfefferkorn's polemics against the Jews fell behind the field and he vanished into history.

18. Johannes Reuchlin (1455–1522)

Born in Pforzheim, in a region particularly susceptible to the intellectual impulses of French and Italian humanism, Reuchlin emerged as the first German humanist of European stature. His juridical studies in Orléans and Poitiers readied him for a brilliant political career. In 1484 he was already a magistrate of the high court of justice in Stuttgart, and from 1502 to 1513 he served as a much-sought-after and influential judge within the Swabian League. He complemented his excellent knowledge of Latin and Greek with the private study of Hebrew. Once he had attained the level of *doctor trilinguis* he began equipping a whole generation of "Christian Hebraists" through his laborious compilation of a grammar, modestly announced as *Rudimenta linguae hebraicae* (1506).

Reuchlin's interest in gaining access to the Hebrew texts resulted from his interest in the cabala, the rabbinic esoteric teaching that seeks to discover the revelation of God as it is hidden in the text of the Old Testament. In his two major works, *De verbo mirificio* (1494;

2d ed., 1514) and *De arte cabalistica* (1517), he gives the cabala a Christian interpretation, regarding it as the veiled Old Testament prophecy of the Messiah Jesus.

From this perspective he defended the value of the Talmudic texts against the charges leveled by *der Tauft Jud* Pfefferkorn. Reuchlin's arguments appeared in his *Augenspiegel,* a tract published for the Easter Mass of Frankfurt in 1511. The resulting controversy with the theologians of Cologne and Dominican inquisitors culminated in his condemnation by the pope in 1520. The great-uncle of Melanchthon thus fell victim to the same climate of fear that claimed the "heretic" Luther, without his ever having adopted the cause of the Reformation itself.

19. Huldreich Zwingli (1484–1531)

Trained in Vienna and Basel in the scholastic tradition of the so-called *via antiqua,* Zwingli came into contact with Wolfgang Capito and Konrad Pellikan in Basel (1502–6). The latter figure belonged at the time to the circle of collaborators on Erasmus's massive edition of Augustine, published by Johannes Amerbach. From 1514 on, Zwingli was an avid disciple of Erasmus. He visited Erasmus from Glarus (1506–16) during the time when Erasmus's Greek New Testament went to press. Called from Einsiedeln to Zurich (1519–31), he became the reformer of that city, although his influence extended far beyond the Swiss Confederacy and southern Germany.

Though not a "Christian Hebraist" like the Reuchlin protégés Pellikan and Capito, Zwingli nonetheless solemnly regarded the Old Testament as the binding Word of God and accorded it copious commentary. As was the case for the other Erasmian disciples and civic reformers, the evangelical reconstruction of the church did not entail for Zwingli a change in his perception of the Jews.

Historical Accountability

Europe in the sixteenth century made a hesitant but nonetheless significant step into the modern age. Although this progress was not felt in all of Europe or in all reaches of European life, just the same, north of the Alps, the cause of human rights made considerable advance. The voices calling for toleration and religious freedom multiplied.[1] Three leading figures in Germany, and as it would turn out, three towers of strength for the entire continent in dark times, each contributed in his own way to this development: Johannes Reuchlin, Erasmus of Rotterdam, and Martin Luther.

This progress, however, left the Jewish communities in Europe for the most part untouched. Tailored exclusively to the needs of a Christian society fragmented by competing social and religious forces, the sixteenth-century ideal of toleration had primarily the character of a Christian restorative, not of a modern, pluralistic ideal. The late fifteenth- and early sixteenth-century dream of toleration made no allowances for unbaptized Jews. In point of fact, the wide diffusion of this ideal was accomplished at the expense of the Jewish population in northern Europe, and above all in Germany, where the social and legal status of the Jews in the empire deteriorated visibly. Reuchlin, Erasmus, and Luther once again played their part in this development, too. And once again, each contributed in his own way.

This immediately raises two questions that will determine the nature and scope of the first part of the present inquiry. First, what justifies mentioning Reuchlin, Erasmus, and Luther, for all their dissimilarity, in the same breath? It appears to be a generally accepted fact, for instance, that Luther publicly broke with Erasmus in 1515, a symbolic act amounting to a formal repudiation of the humanistic movement. Further, how is it possible that each of these three historical figures could have been so divided within as to embrace such wholly incompatible positions—to advocate toleration while venting anti-Jewish sentiments?

Anyone today who wishes to trace the historical confrontation between the Jewish communities and the European society of the sixteenth century cannot complain of a scarcity of source materials or of reliable interpretations. Still, there is reason to complain, for we are burdened with a depressing mass of books that only on the surface appear to address our topic, when in fact they simply use the misery of the Jews in the sixteenth century to document the decisive role of economic factors. In this strain of scholarship, economic conditions are held to be not only contributing, but wholly determining factors of Christian-Jewish relations in early modern Europe. The authors of such studies pay all due respect to "accounts receivable," but contribute nothing toward a genuine account of the historical riddle why, if money explains all, the great Augsburg banking house of Fugger was merely cursed, while the Jews were driven away.

To be sure, economic factors and pressures must be taken into account,[2] but they should never determine an inquiry. Such causes are significant clues that can help detect a whole vital configuration of human motives describing the acts of individuals and groups. Consider the example of the pamphlet literature, with its strident calls for reform, aimed at the man in the street. These documents betray obvious signs of hatred for the Jews. Publicists, on the other hand, who stood close to the emperor or to those princes who levied protective taxes on the Jews, tended to voice friendlier sentiments. Here the effects of economic motivations are easily discernible. In general, though, the historical record is so unwieldy and so contradictory that it proves impossible to fix any absolute demarcation between the exceptions and the rule. Hatred of the Jews did not exist apart from protection of the Jews; these were two sides of the same coin, or rather, confusing welter that was shaped by a multiplicity of motivations conditioning either side. In light of these considerations, we should guard against isolating economic pressures from religious convictions on the assumption that such a neat, clinical separation would allow for a simpler explanation of Europe's behavior toward the Jews in terms of one or the other of the "uniquely determinant" factors.

All of the considerations mentioned above and all other imaginable methodological problems are, however, eclipsed by yet another difficulty, often tacit if not suppressed, that burdens any utterance on the subject: we are writing history in the wake of the Nazi massacre. As a rule, historians acknowledge at least the public obligation to present an unprejudiced picture of history. We react sharply whenever one of our colleagues in the historical guild fails to attain this lofty academic ideal. And yet we all stand so spellbound by that nightmarish horror that it is difficult, in this shadowy realm of history, to make clear judgments and correct verdicts while groping for the boundary between aggressive accusation and escapist apology.

When a historian proceeds on the assumption that his first and foremost task is to serve as the final advocate and defense counsel of the dead, he cannot help but confound his position with his person, his academic gown with his conscience. And if he feels that his second task is to assume the role of public prosecutor, he may find himself unable to evade the moral pressure of indicting the past, lest it repeat itself in the future. The historian actually discharges both offices at once when he summons the available sources to the stand to give their eyewitness testimony. At this point, as plaintiff, counsel, and finally even as judge, his abilities are stretched to their human limits; he may neither portray himself as an enlightened mind at the expense of history nor, out of excessive reverence for the past, may he invoke the "spirit of the times" as a mitigating circumstance. These constraints are valid whether his judgments are about single agents, say, Martin Luther, or about that era of timid efforts in the direction of toleration in northern Europe, which is widely celebrated as the finest fruit of Renaissance humanism.

At the beginning of this century, enlightened scholars unanimously endorsed a scale of historical values and a corresponding set of roles that today, under the impact of our most recent history, have virtually established themselves as the orthodox canon. Thus, the loyal subject Reuchlin steps forward as the father of Jewish emancipation, the German nationalist Luther as the bigoted anti-Semite, and the European Erasmus as the paragon of tolerance and the champion of human dignity. Even the slightest deviations and revisions evoke suspicions of heresy. On this stage where history is overcome act by act, the roles have long been assigned and duly performed. A respectable consensus controls what the solid German citizen has to profess and what the incorrigible German—at least today, privately—believes. In retrospect the re-eruption of Christianity in the sixteenth century shows, on the other hand, how reckless it is to pin hatred of the Jews on German "blood and soil." We not only have a right to more accurate information and to less

15

cosmetic history; our society stands in need of a collective anamnesis, a reassessment, however painful that might be, of the birth and growth of its modern age. For what is at stake is not a German past that, once overcome, will release its grip on the present and deliver us into the future.

NOTES

1. Erich Hassinger, *Religiöse Toleranz im 16. Jahrhundert. Motive— Argumente—Formen der Verwirklichung,* lectures for the Aeneas-Silvius Foundation delivered at the University of Basel 6 (Basel 1966). Hans R. Guggisberg, "Veranderingen in de argumenten voor religieuze tolerantie en godsdienstvrijheid in de zestiende en zeventiende eeuw," *Bijdragen en Mededelingen betreffende de Geschiendenis der Nederlanden* 91 (1966): 177–95.

2. See Stuart Jenks's pioneering essay, "Judenverschuldung und Verfol-gung von Juden im 14. Jahrhundert: Franken bis 1349," *Vierteljahrschrift für Sozial- und Wirtschaftsgeschichte* 65 (1978): 309–65.

THE JEWS AT THE THRESHOLD
OF THE MODERN AGE

Whatever comes into the heads or dreams of these people
[the reformers] they give to the world for evangelical
riffraff to read. For instance, right now there is this
superficially learned children's preacher with the hoof of
the golden calf in his flank, who presumes to defend
the bloodthirsty Jews, saying that it is not true and
not plausible that they murder Christian children or use
their blood, to the mockery and ridicule of the
authorities and all of Christendom . . .

Johannes Eck
Ains Judenbüechlins Verlegung
1542, fol. A IV^r

1

Strange Bedfellows

In the historical perspective of the nineteenth and early twentieth centuries, the Renaissance and the Reformation appeared to be kindred movements that jointly guided Europe out of the medieval patterns of life and thought, and into the modern era. Today, no self-respecting scholar can afford to range Reuchlin, Erasmus, and Luther along a single, unbroken line of development that leads from the "darkness" of the Middle Ages to the "progress" of the modern age. Cognizant of the unquestionable existence of mutual influences and momentary alliances, we have also learned to be sensitive to the in part quite diverse mainsprings and objectives of those movements of renewal that today are so neatly compartmentalized under the labels "Renaissance" and "Reformation."

At this point we confront the dilemma of all historiography, namely, the predictable rule that what is perceived by contemporaries to be the focal points of historical moment for a given epoch will inevitably differ from, or even conflict with, the findings of a later historical assessment. Thus, it should not surprise us if the dividing line between "Renaissance" and "Reformation" was for sixteenth-century contemporaries unclear, even invalid. One of the most cultivated, productive, and widely read of the early champions for a renewal of church and society, Johannes Eberlin of Günzburg, would have rejected today's historical compartmentalization as a bizarre artificiality or even as a falsification of history. In his polemical tract *The Fifteen Confederates,* Eberlin, a Franciscan monk who was driven from Ulm in 1521 for his evangelical convictions, depicted Reuchlin and Erasmus as Luther's allies. He regarded this pair as founding fathers who had "laid the cornerstone of all salvation."[1] The kernel of Eberlin's picture is not without historical truth, though on closer inspection we find that the differences between Luther and Reuchlin far outweighed the shared similarities.

Reuchlin (d. 1522), Erasmus (d. 1536), and Luther (d. 1546) differ from one another already in one, only apparently trivial, regard: the three men reached the peak of their intellectual powers in three successive decades. But rarely have decades been so swiftly estranged. In these thiry years, Europe was to withstand a period of dramatic reversals and radical changes in the very fabric of its existence.

Not only age but also origin play a role. Reuchlin was a Swabian. Despite his exotic education in the French universities at Paris, Orléans, and Poitiers, and despite his Italian sojourn, he remained bound to his native Swabia, which compassed the region between Pforzheim, his birthplace, Stuttgart, the capital of Württemberg, and the university town of Tübingen. Until 1513 he discharged his first official function as a judge in the Swabian League,[2] a major power in the empire that earned even greater respect when it succeeded in driving Duke Ulrich, the free cities' foe, from Württemberg. The loyalties of the League judge were pledged to southern Germany and the emperor. In this way, the learned professor of classical languages combined his love for philology with a fine sense for the political dimensions of jurisprudence.

Erasmus, on the other hand, never received a legal training nor did he ever express an interest in juridical questions or political structures. In no way bound to the land of his birth, the Netherlandish county of Holland, he instead preferred to travel in the swift-moving world of European learned letters and ideas. The stopping points on his scholarly pilgrimage were always provisional, never a permanent home. Home was, as he liked to put it, "wherever my library happens to be." His residence of choice was along the Rhine, the pulsing artery of news and culture for which he constantly yearned.[3] In 1518, in a letter to the Saxon Elector Frederick, Reuchlin nominated candidates for the professorship of Greek in Wittenberg and made no bones about the fact that Erasmus could never even pass for a German: "In Germany, I know of no better candidate for the chair in Greek than Melanchthon"—his great-nephew—"excepting Erasmus, but he is Dutch."[4] Erasmus was never regarded a German—he was what he was, a European.

Martin Luther, too, was a much-traveled man, with one major qualification: except for a single journey over the Alps, occasioned by business with Rome, he never ventured beyond the borders of the

German empire. After his condemnation by the emperor at Worms (1521) and until the end of his life, his movements were even further restricted, first to areas within the limits of Saxony, and later even more narrowly to evangelical districts. His writings crossed oceans; he himself preferred to travel on solid ground and highways. He harbored a lifelong distrust for rivers. When they suddenly swelled and flooded their banks, Luther suspected devilry that was aimed at impeding his travel, or at rendering his return to Wittenberg more of a hardship.

The differences between these three figures naturally run deeper still, until they reach that decisive point where profession and calling converge. Reuchlin was the learned jurist, the first German Hebraist and, generally speaking, the first German scholar to bear comparison with the great Italian savants—a homemade Pico della Mirandola.[5] Erasmus was the Hellenist par excellence who occasioned the church the same degree of discomfiture through his edition of the Greek New Testament (1516) as did Luther through his theses on indulgences (1517). Luther was the profound and prophetic biblical theologian in whose able grasp the new *instrumentarium* produced by Reuchlin (in Hebrew) and Erasmus (in Greek) came to provide a firm basis for sound doctrine and the proclamation of the gospel.

In view of this historical constellation, one indeed has the right to talk about a triumvirate. But this revolutionary, fresh orientation to the sources, rightly described by Eberlin of Günzburg as the goal common to all three men, was not what brought them together; rather, it was what set them apart. Their respective scriptural readings, though unanimously based on a preference for the original biblical text over the Latin Vulgate, whose authority until then had remained undisputed, diverged at essential points. Linguistic equipments alone drove the scholarly labors of each of these three down divergent paths. Of the three, Reuchlin was the only truly *trilinguis*. He was fully competent in Hebrew, Greek, and classical Latin. Erasmus pursued the Hebrew language for a time, but soon gave it up, citing as reasons the brevity of life and the pressure of his numerous research projects.[6] Luther, on the other hand, thoroughly devoted himself to Hebrew and learned to value it uniquely. More than any other language, Hebrew struck him as unaffected and powerfully direct: *"lingua Ebraica est omnium optima . . . ac purissima . . .* It has a color of its own."[7] He contrasted the unspeculative clarity of Hebrew with Greek,[8] but never acquired the easy familiarity that Erasmus and Melanchthon had with the language of Plato and Aristotle—a familiarity which later became a matter of course in scholarly circles. Luther's real gift clearly lay in his mastery of German, and even the wit and bite of his Latin writings betray his inventive play with his mother tongue.

All these differences of period, origin, vocation, and training were ignored by Eberlin no less than by successive learned generations. Striking as they were, the differences were easily overshadowed by the more visible and spectacular controversy that drew Reuchlin, Erasmus, and Luther into coalition against the "Obscure Men," the proponents of medieval scholasticism who themselves had joined forces with the Dominican watchdog of orthodoxy, the inquisitor of Cologne, Jacob, Hochstraten (d. 1527). This latter alliance, conservative, restorationist, and sworn to in the name of the Vulgate, was so deeply and inseparably bound up with the centers of power that it could mete out a comparable fate to all three. Reuchlin and Luther were condemned in 1520. In 1559, after decades of hostility, Pope Paul IV put the works of Erasmus on the Index of forbidden books where they continued to appear, selectively and variously, in later, updated lists.[9]

With this we arrive at an essential point of contact that concerns not the foundations these three men shared as a lowest common denominator, but the common effect and reaction they produced. Only provisionally, and then only in a very well-structured authoritarian state, can censorship prevent freely conducted research from striking deeper roots. Just the same, we should not be misled by this shared fate of defamation and condemnation: Reuchlin, Erasmus, and Luther did not form a common front in the battle for the universally desired renewal of the church. Their individual motivations and objectives were too hopelessly at odds to permit such a claim. If Reuchlin occupied himself with Hebrew ideas to the extent and detail that he did,[10] it was in order to prove the superiority and the universality of Christian faith, a task which he thought lay beyond the technics of scholasticism. Erasmus's interests shifted gradually away from the anti-scholastic and anti-clerical satires of his early, critical phase; he feared for the cause of the *bonae litterae,* the classical program of education that, obviating the need for strife and discord, would create the conditions for humanitarian improvement, starting at the level of the individual and ascending from there to the church and society as a whole. Luther took an early stance against the *infelices Colonienses,* the unholy scholastics of Cologne,[11] though his sights were trained on other targets than those cherished enemies of Reuchlin[12] and Erasmus. He picked his quarrel

21

not with the professors who turned a deaf ear to the classical way, but with those who were infatuated with their robes and degrees, whom he collectively derided as *magistri nostri;* it was not their deficiencies in training or education but the remoteness of their theology from the Bible that triggered his assault. In 1522 Luther unceremoniously distanced himself from his contemporary converts to education. His battle with the scholastics has nothing to do with their shortage of rhetorical finesse or depth of learning. In this regard, he granted, "I am just as unpolished as they—*sum et ego barbarus.*"[13]

The grounds for portraying the triumvirate as a closed intellectual phalanx—the received view, sustained and enshrined in teachings and legends—are obviously unsound. Once the incongruities are left aside, there does remain a common bond—the visionary confidence all three had that a renewed, impartial, and scrupulous study of the biblical sources would provide the key to wisdom, which would in turn unveil truth in its pure condition and revive both church and society.

For all its boldness and clear-sighted focus that points into the modern age, this vision goes hand in hand, in all three cases, with an anti-Judaism that undoubtedly can be linked up to traditional, medieval images of hatred, but that should not by any means be underestimated as a mere relic from the Middle Ages. Anti-Judaism is the concerted assault by humanism and the Reformation against all externalizations of inner values; it is the triumph over the dead letter in the name of the living spirit. Anti-Judaism in this form is destined to become an integral component of the reform program of the sixteenth century. In the struggle for the renewal of church and society, Jews and Judaism will be adduced as comprehensible and unambiguous proofs of the spiritual chaos of the time. Although the boundaries to the later anti-Semitism are clearly marked out, the crossovers and points of transgression have equally clearly been mapped in.

This survey of their positions toward Jews and Judaism throws an unexpected and unwelcome light on the question: In what ways were Reuchlin, Erasmus, and Luther ahead of their time and precursors of the Enlightenment, or even of our own age? The movement toward religious toleration celebrated later with such heady pride, sprang from beginnings that are in fact most sobering. Even the sixteenth century, so self-consciously at odds with the Middle Ages, did not to any measurable degree surpass its counterpart where the Jews were concerned. The awakening to reform and Reformation tended, if anything, to further the demarcation of the true Christendom on all its flanks. It is our own unfounded pride in a liberating modernity and an achieved emancipation that has made us susceptible, in the flush of success, to glossing over the dark limits of toleration.

2

Johannes Reuchlin:
Reform or Expulsion

The *Letters of Obscure Men* (1515, 1517) have always fascinated. With this parody of a scholastic fossil that had been rendered obsolete by humanist minds, the educated German world proclaimed its rejection of the Latin Middle Ages.

A byproduct of the controversy that surrounded the confiscation and burning of Judaic writings in 1507, the *Letters* are also suggestive of the larger battle waged between the two educational authorities, humanism and scholasticism, or as the *Letters* would have it, between education and authority. This front, drawn as it was in the heat of battle, ultimately collapses when viewed in a cooler light and against the general European background. Paul Oskar Kristeller[14] and Charles Trinkhaus[15] have demonstrated how the medieval roots of Renaissance humanism reach back into the citadels of scholastic thought, into Thomism and nominalism.

To appreciate the true extent of the debt owed by the most prominent humanists to the scholastics, we need to go back to the beginnings. Johannes Reuchlin, at least, was conscious of his roots and always intent on synthesis. But even Reuchlin had no illusions about the guilt that had opened between tradition and educational progress and was widening around the sensitive and critical issue of biblical texts. He was prepared for the inevitable consequence of his tampering with the hallowed authority of the Vulgate, the textbook for theology and church dogma. Recently, though, the thesis has been advanced that the "real" controversy was located in a totally different arena; on this view, the "Obscure Men" from Cologne assailed Reuchlin less for his humanistic exertions than for his Jewish sympathies: "The anti-Reuchlinists were comprised of a disparate group of anti-Semites from many walks of life; they included some scholastics, but also a few humanists and even several kings."[16] This thesis about Reuchlin's Jewish sympathies needs careful restriction: Reuchlin's undertakings were not motivated by pro-Jewish, let alone pro-Semitic considerations.

With this last remark we have entered sensitive ground since neither consensus nor clarity govern the use and meaning of these two concepts within the framework of sixteenth-century experience. The language of our sources is not to be trusted blindly. Even a citation bare of commentary is sufficient for eloquent distortion. Much of what later generations condemn as racism can easily be part of the vocabulary that, in the context of the sixteenth century, was a historical given and says little or nothing about the revolutionary changes and breakthroughs of the age. How, then, are we to measure the degrees of anti-Judaism and determine its significance for a world we can never truly inhabit—a world we must visit as foreigners forever? This was a religious world that viewed truth as indivisible, banned deviation as error, and dreaded patent heresy as blasphemy fatal to a life with God. This world oscillated back and forth between conscience-racking options. It could not decide whether to accept the inevitability of the last resort—forced, large-scale conversions—or to interpret the failed peaceful mission to the Jews as proof of the punishment of God and as a verification of Christian truth. George Santayana's epigrammatic definition of the fanatic comes to mind: someone who redoubles his zeal whenever he has lost sight of his goal. Christian anti-Jewish fanaticism, which showed itself incapable of deciding between these two options—mass conversion and mass expulsion—is as incomprehensible as it is fascinating. What to modern eyes looks like an all-too-familiar fanaticism in fact conceals nuances and new answers that only immersion in the sources and acclimation to the age can bring to light.

What are the reliable symptoms that justify reference to a sixteenth-century prototype of anti-Semitism? Confiscation of Jewish books, or is the protection tax that was levied on Jewish communities enough? Neurotic fear or, worse, aggression-precipitating slander, like rumors about desecrations of the host or ritual murder stories whereby Jews were alleged to have procured Christian blood for the healing of their own illnesses? What constitutes evidence of a "liberal attitude"? The willingness to waive the death sentence for Jews and settle for expulsion, while perhaps "even" foregoing the confiscation of all moveable effects?[17] These questions, perfectly suited to the time, warn against the undifferentiated application of the massively charged term "anti-Semitism."

Not the famous "Reuchlin controversy" with the "Obscure Men," but its occasion is relevant to the Jewish question in the sixteenth century: the renewed inquisitional attack upon the Talmud on the grounds that this collection of rabbinical law and tradition was both blasphemous and seditious. The public debate around Reuchlin was ignited by the appearance of his *Augenspiegel* in Tübingen in 1511, a polemical work in which Reuchlin condemned the indiscriminate destruction of the Talmudic texts. The battle of the quill was on, but the focus shifted immediately: instead of the Talmudic dispute, Reuchlin's orthodoxy was now put at issue. Whether Reuchlin's orthodoxy ever really was an issue will have to be determined by examining the relevant works in the Reuchlin corpus.[18] For this reason we omit from our discussion the two volumes of his *Epistolae obscurorum virorum,* published in 1511 by Crotus Rubeanus and in 1517 by Ulrich von Hutten. His compact Latin lexicon, the *Vocabularius breviloquus* (Basel, 1478) is equally silent on the matter of the Jews. This leaves the extremely important *De verbo mirifico* (Basel, 1494); *De rudimentis hebraicis* (Pforzheim, 1506), the first Hebrew grammar; and the *Opinion,* a statement advising against the confiscation of Hebrew books, presented to the emperor in 1510 and published the following year in the *Augenspiegel.*[19]

Let us take up these works in chronological order, beginning with the *De verbo mirifico (The Wondrous Word),*[20] to determine the stance it takes toward the Jews. The *De verbo mirifico* has been variously interpreted in the course of time: as a demonstration of the need for learning Hebrew, as a defense of the Christian cabala, as the personal expression of Reuchlin's mystical proclivities, and—most recently and most illuminating of all,[21]—as a program for retrieving the divine gift of the occult sciences, which would in turn enable men to master the powers of nature with the ancillary aid of the cabala. By "cabala" Reuchlin understood a method that, secretly transmitted and "until recently" accessible only to Jewish erudites, was designed to unlock the mystery of God's revelation and even God's very name from their occulted source—in and behind the letters of the Old Testament. This revelation, once grasped, points beyond the Old Testament into the New, thus both confirming the Jewish Bible and leaving it behind as the antiquated book of the old covenant.

The substance of the treatise, to be presented here in its abstract lineaments, is deftly and graphically represented in a "religious colloquy," a device that is also the center of attraction in his work on the cabala, *De arte cabalistica* (1517). The occasion is a dispute among Sidon, the born Epicurean and stand-in for pagan philosophy; Baruch, the learned Jew; and Capnion, Reuchlin's spokesman for the learned Christian view. Within this conversational frame, or rather, contention over truth (*sectarum controversia*)[22]—thus recalling, but fundamentally different from, Lessing's manifesto on toleration *Nathan der Weise*—Capnion proves the superiority of the Christian faith while demanding and securing the repentance[23] of Sidon and Baruch. The victory is sealed through baptismal and purification rituals. Just as Sidon must abjure Epicurus and the godless search for pleasure, Baruch must relinquish the Talmud and discard all objections to the Messiah Christ. "Let this be the way of your conversion: You, Baruch, turn away from the Talmud, and you, Sidon, from Epicurus (*resipiscentia vestra haec esto: a Thalmudim, Baruchia, tuque Sidoni ab Epicuro . . . receditote*); let yourselves be cleansed in baptismal waters (*lavamini, mundi estote*)."[24]

Clearly, this is not a crude attempt at conversion through indictment, which leaves the opponent convicted of either stupidity or obstinance. *De arte cabalistica* constitutes a real step toward Lessing and the Enlightenment where the religion of the opponent will be taken seriously and recognized for its germ of truth. The bare form, to be sure, recalls the medieval disputations between Christians and Jews; but these, unlike Reuchlin's work, were staged as mock trials. The disputation of the learned humanist is essentially an introduction to the fine art of the *magus* who, from his superior vantage point, succeeds in contemplating the disparate elements of truth in their original unity. Reuchlin is unquestionably now the Christian magician who discovers that Christ was the first and only unveiler of the truth concerning Gentiles and Jews.

It is precisely this plank of his argument that separates Capnion-Reuchlin from Lessing, and explains the otherwise unfathomable: Reuchlin's combination of respect for the Hebrew language and deference to the cabalistic method with a flat rejection of the Talmud. In a single, unexpected blow, Reuchlin shatters the modern image of him and illumines the distance that still remains to be covered before the Enlightenment can be reached: "You Jews have perverted the holy mysteries, and for this reason you murmur your prayers in vain; in vain you call on God, whom you fail to venerate as he would have you. You flatter yourselves with your concocted ceremonies and persecute us, who truly serve God, with immortal hatred."[25]

This conjunction of scholarly respect and hostility in the name of Christ should not be lightly dismissed as an inconsistency produced, perhaps inevitably, by a late German pupil of an Italian import, the cabala. Reuchlin here is pursuing an already well-worn argument, one, for instance, that the converted Jew and cabalist Flavius Mithri-

27

dates had openly advanced in a Good Friday sermon before the pope and cardinals in Rome in 1481: "The Jews conceal their occult science and refuse to make it public, lest we come to have a share in it. But I, Flavius Mithridates, am not deceived in this, and know perfectly well what great fruits Christianity has reaped from those Jews who were converted to the gospel."[26]

In his "open letter of protest," the Tütsch missive, composed in German in 1505, Reuchlin makes this indignation thematic. He describes the "misery" of the Jews (their exile) as a punishment from God for their collective guilt. The Jews have been so utterly smitten with blindness that they now are incapable of finding the route to repentance. "The way to repentance is contrition and suffering,"[27] in other words, conversion, and ultimately, attachment to the Christian church. Only the learned Jew will discover this option, only the wise initiate of the cabalistic mysteries will come to grasp how the Hebrew characters for the name of the Almightly mean *Jeschu*, that is, Jesus. This treatise[28] is in essence a practical application of *De verbo mirifico*. Baruch's recantation is no longer described as a simple change of mind, but as a categorical change of faith. Because the misery of the Jews is a God-given punishment, not an injustice attributable to men, the Jews' only hope for escaping divine judgment lies in conversion.

Reuchlin closes with an allusion to the Good Friday prayer for the *perfidi Judaei*, the "perfidious Jews": "I pray to God that he enlighten the Jews and show them the way to the right belief, that they might be delivered from their diabolical captivity. As soon as they acknowledge Jesus to be the true Messiah, their condition will take a turn for the better, both in this world and in the world to come. Amen."[29] Again, this possibility is open only to a select and fortunate few, namely, those Jews who are conversant with the secrets of the wonder-working Word.

The informative preface to the *De rudimentis hebraicis*, completed on 5 March 1506, contains a compressed summary of Reuchlin's previous discoveries and a prophetic proclamation of events that would both establish and damage his reputation as *Praeceptor Germaniae*, the title and honor he finally bequeathed to his great-nephew, the Wittenberg reformer Philipp Melanchthon. Reuchlin declares his resolve to defend the indispensability of a Hebrew training against all concerned educational authorities, against the scholastics, the Jews, and even against the humanists. Behind this aggressive stance is the conviction that Bible study had been done devastating harm not only at the hands of the scholastic "sophists," but at the hands of the students of rhetoric and poetry as well.[30] The *litterati* may well be of the opinion that his interest in grammatical questions is but a preoccupation with *puerilia,* child's play not very befitting a man of learning.[31] The study of grammar, however, has always been the real foundation of philosophy; and for the same reason, knowledge of Hebrew is the essential prerequisite for any serious treatment of the cabala.[32]

Reuchlin depicts his isolated position with a candid realism: the humanists shower him with derision and punish him with disdain, the Jews reject him, and the Sophists fall upon him like rabid dogs.[33] How monstrous! (so runs their hue and cry), the man is so impudent as to criticize the holy Vulgate and to question the inspired translation that the holy Jerome produced and the great Lyra commentated![34] Reuchlin's estimate of the dangers in his undertaking and the power of his adversaries proved to be historically accurate. The following statement combines the metered ring of rhetoric with the persuasive power of undaunted truth: "Although I venerate Jerome as an angel and highly esteem Lyra as a master, I bow before the truth as before God" (*Quamquam enim Hieronymum sanctum veneror ut angelum, et Lyram colo ut magistrum, tamen adoro veritatem ut deum*).[35]

This show of independence, daring in any age, has become the basis of all genuine historical investigation. From it follows the necessity of evaluating the great master himself by his own maxim. The modern picture of Reuchlin as a friend of the Jews, for all its accessibility, simply does not stand up. Reuchlin was firmly convinced of the collective guilt of the Jews, and he had no intention of challenging the righteousness of their punishment by God, their present and eternal misery. This punishment could be stayed only in the case of a slender elite, those few who were willing to renounce the Talmud and to prostrate themselves before the Christian cabala, the Jewish witness to the Christian faith.

Although Reuchlin openly avowed his great indebtedness to the "highly cultivated and well-read" physician of Emperor Frederick III, the Jew Jacob ben Jehiel Loans, from whom he received his introduction to the Hebrew alphabet,[36] he knew better than to expect from the Jews any positive reaction to his having finally deciphered the Hebrew language.[37] The Christianization of Hebrew, Reuchlin reasoned in his preface to the third part of his grammar, is all the more necessary, since "our German Jews refuse to teach Christians their language, whether out of malice or incompetence. To back their position, they appeal to a proscription in the Talmud."[38] Reuchlin himself formulated the principle that would soon move his opponents into action against the Jews: the Talmud stands between the Jews and their conversion.

When the Swabian judge handed down an opinion against the confiscation of Jewish books, he argued, as Guido Kisch has convincingly demonstrated,[39] on the basis of Roman law, the *Codex Iustinianus*. In apparent contradiction with his contemporaries' picture of the Jew as enemy, Reuchlin the jurist concludes that Jews are not slaves, but rather *concives,* co-citizens; not heretics in the sense that has meaning in church law, but a sect to be tolerated in virtue of imperial law. For Christians, this legal consideration admits of only one conclusion: Jewish books may not be confiscated without prior inspection, and Jews should be converted through instruction, "through reasoned disputation, gently and kindly."[40]

This piece of legal counsel earned Reuchlin much hatred in his own time, and the suspicion that the undutiful magistrate had "most certainly" been suborned to do the commonwealth some deliberate harm. In modern studies, Reuchlin's opinion is hailed as a record of enlightenment and toleration that towers over the limits of the sixteenth century and points toward the modern age of emancipatory activism. This view is so firmly anchored that nothing will render it concordant with, and thus innocuous to, our diagnosis of Reuchlin's fundamental critique of the Talmud and the charges of collective guilt he brought against the Jews. Naturally, the historian always has available his panacea: by accusing his author of inconsistency or timidity, both author and historian slip out from under the yoke of responsibility. In the face of the clear-cut testimony of our sources, however, neither relativization nor harmonization will do, but only—and here we join company with Reuchlin—differentiation: Jews are citizens of two worlds, fellow citizens of the imperial realm, and adversaries in the kingdom of God. Reuchlin here is in search of a two-kingdoms theory, just as Luther will later distinguish between the kingdom of God and the kingdom of earth, though without in the last analysis upgrading the political status of the Jews. For Reuchlin, Jews are "inimical to our faith," while at the same time "*concives*," legal equals and thus fellow citizens "under one civil law and one civil peace." If, however, they fail to show any signs of improvement—if, for example, they do not refrain from usury, the distinction between citizen and "fellow citizen" will prove to be definitive, and religious animosity decisive. The Jews in this case will have forfeited their residence permit and must be expelled: "Make improvements or out!" (*reformandi seu expellendi*).[41]

This Janus-faced policy also explains Reuchlin's apparent retreat. To the charge that he was a heretic and financed by the Jews, he replied in his *Augenspiegel* (Tübingen, 1511) that his defense of Jewish texts had been fundamentally misconstrued. Neither did he have any qualms about endorsing the then-currently popular solution and recommending that the "heretical and blasphemous portions" of the Talmud be confiscated and kept under lock and key in Christian libraries.[42] This reformulation enabled Reuchlin to accord respect to imperial law, to satisfy the churchly Inquisition, . . . and still preserve the interests of research and teaching.[43]

The *Augenspiegel* is a trustworthy commentary on the judicial opinion that Reuchlin submitted one year before. The spokesman for the civil rights of Jews was never brought to his knees through intimidation. He remained true to his program from the very beginning: his defense was not meant for impenitent Jew or the Jewish Talmud, but rather for the gaining unblocked access to the sources of the Christian cabala. Reuchlin linked the Jewish right to individual protection with the Christian right to protect its own society. Required were, therefore, repentance, conversion, and "signs of improvement." For the obstinate, there remained expulsion.

3

Johannes Pfefferkorn:
The Shrill Voice of a Convert

For over a century, scholarship has taken practically no notice of the tracts of Johannes Pfefferkorn (1469–1522/23).[44] The angry diatribes of this fanatic seemed sufficiently well known and adequately documented. The Jew Pfefferkorn, christened in 1505 under the name of Johannes, published his *Mirror of Jews (Judenspiegel)* in both German and Latin in 1507, in Nuremberg and Cologne.[45] This was followed by a spate of pamphlets, which were reprinted in several cities: *The Jewish Confessions* (1508), *How the Blind Jews Worship Their Easter* (1509), and a first culmination point, *The Foe of the Jews,*[46] complete with an epigram by the Cologne professor Ortwin Gratius (1509), who as addressee of the *Letters of Obscure Men* and a prominent anti-Reuchlinist, was soon to become the target of general scorn in the learned world.

In the *Judenspiegel* of 1507, Pfefferkorn presented his fateful demand: the Talmudic books should be impounded and burned. This is one of the few passages cited by Reuchlin's biographer, Ludwig Geiser, and is generally the only word of Pfefferkorn to have been lodged in the memory of posterity.[47] The first pages of the *Judenspiegel* immediately make clear why Pfefferkorn's modern readers have lost all incentive to read further. With the hatred of one searching for new intellectual and emotional roots, the convert tears himself free of his past. Supported by the Vulgate, the church-authorized Bible text that Reuchlin was just submitting to critical examination, Pfefferkorn wished to convert his "brothers after the flesh" through that admixture of argumentation and indictment which by then was routine from centuries of Christian missions to the Jews.

Four points deserve special notice. Pfefferkorn's goal was to enlist the aid of Christians, notably princes and city fathers, in sweeping clear all obstacles that stood in the way of a Jewish conversion—the true work of a good Christian. To this end, all Hebrew books with the exception of the Old Testament must be seized and burned.[48] "On the face of it, it will be objected," Pfefferkorn replied in anticipation of later criticisms,

> that my proposal is as imprudent as it is immoral, since I seem to be recommending that the authorities take illegal and unjust (*contra ius et fas*) action against the Jews' possessions. And yet I firmly maintain: this is not a matter of stealing anything from anybody; on the contrary, the Jews stand to gain something thereby. But first allow me this question: Why are the Jews so pitilessly persecuted by you Christians? As everybody knows, they have to pay high taxes for public protection and for the guarantee of law. They are burdened like mules when by rights they ought to be as free as birds in a forest. The argument whereby you seek to justify your greed, namely, that this is a way of forcing their conversion, is not very convincing. You want it to seem as if whatever the Jews are compelled to suffer is for their own good. Why shouldn't you this once make an exception and do something that, though it bring you no gain, at least opens for them the way to eternal salvation?[49]

The first point which emerges from this passage is that Pfefferkorn's "plan of salvation," to which he owes his place in our histories, was integrated with a bold critique of the view that Jews could be arbitrarily taxed and exploited[50] as the state's *Kammerknechte* ("chamber servants").[51]

A second remarkable fact is that before the outbreak of the Reuchlin controversy, Pfefferkorn had sought out Reuchlin as an authority and esteemed Hebraist, and had done more than simply observe him at work in his study.[52] In fact, Pfefferkorn's view was fundamentally that of Reuchlin in his *De verbo mirifico*. In the cabala, the Jews possess the key to the divine revelation, and in the letters of the Hebrew Scriptures is stored the wisdom that is capable of unfolding the mysteries of creation.[53] This is also the reason why Pfefferkorn inveighed so heavily against the University of Mainz's opinion that had recommended the wholesale confiscation of Jewish books, the five books of Moses included.[54]

Third, Pfefferkorn's confiscation plans were bound up with the anticipation that an extensive conversion of Jews would take place before Judgment Day could arrive. The church had already discovered the connection between Jewish conversion and Judgment Day in Paul's Epistle to the Romans (11:25f.): blindness has afflicted the Jews, until the Gentiles can be brought into the fold. "And so all Israel shall be saved." As Pfefferkorn saw matters, all signs point to the speedy end. It is dead certain, a violent cataclysm is imminent:

injustice is spreading like fire; God's punitive justice cannot be stayed for much longer.[55] But before the final advent, the Jews will convert to the true faith; he himself, Pfefferkorn, stands on the mere threshold of a vast movement. Conversion of the Jews is, however, only possible if they are handled "correctly." This includes, among other measures, "naturally" also the confiscation of Jewish books, which after all only serves their best interests, their salvation.[56]

In his anticipation of the Last Days, Pfefferkorn did not stand alone. For Luther, too, the end was in sight, though he did not by any means interpret the conversion of Jews mentioned in Paul's Letter to the Romans as a mass event. Conversion for Luther applied to individuals, not groups, and it never happened by force. Pfefferkorn and Luther shared with their Christian contemporaries a fundamental ambivalence toward two conflicting obligations: the mission to the Jews, and the protection of Christianity from the Jews. This ambivalence of obligation was reflected in the inability to decide between two options: whether to come down squarely in favor of a concerted effort at conversion, or else to allow the so strongly felt hatred of Jews to play itself out. In the section on Luther below, we will want to question the reformer about this pervasive indecision. It is worth noting at this point that the thrust of Luther's pamphlet *Jesus Christ Was Born a Jew* (1523)[57]—his criticism of the way Jews were being treated, and his plea for a "new objectivity" toward the Jewish question—is significantly different from the thrust of Pfefferkorn's program.[58] Luther never counted on an extensive and comprehensive conversion of Jews.[59] And though at first sight this seems a purely quantitative distinction, it has in fact far-reaching consequences for that complex matrix of issues and emotions which was built around the two ideas: Jewish conversion and the world's end. The successful Jewish mission represented a first phase along the way toward the millennium, the expected reign of peace at the end of time. The obstinacy of the Jews consequently stood like a belligerent roadblock along this path to the final breakthrough to the reign of peace, the ultimate realization of law and justice, of prosperity and the common good. A Jew-free world, on the other hand, was *not* in Luther's view a precondition for the coming kingdom of God.

A fourth and final remark will lead us from Cologne on the eve of the Reformation to Nuremberg and Ingolstadt during the 1540s and the new escalation in anti-Jewish feeling. Pfefferkorn had criticized and berated the Christians in no uncertain terms—and this has never been added to his portfolio—for damaging their own cause through giving credence to the widely circulating stories about Jewish ritual murders. With these old wives' tales about Jews who allegedly kill little children for the medicinal properties of their Christian blood, "we are making fools of ourselves and exposing the Christian faith to ridicule and contempt."[60]

Early in 1529 an anonymous tract on this explosive subject appeared: *Whether It Be True and Credible That the Jews Secretly Strangulate Christian Children and Make Use of Their Blood.*[61] Today there is no doubt that this document was the work of Andreas Osiander (1498–1552),[62] the reformer of Nuremberg, the chief stronghold of the Lutheran Reformation in the southern half of the empire. The following year (1530), this city openly entered the lists of the Reformation by subscribing to the Augsburg Confession. Osiander had read Pfefferkorn and found him sufficiently important to involve him in the defense of the Jews. Pfefferkorn's cautions served the Nuremberg reformer as a basis for developing his own argument in the controversy over the ritual murder issue. In Osiander's eyes, this sort of indictment was pure slander, mere rabble-rousing grounded not on facts, but on envy and greed.

Osiander dared to confront agitation with information. To begin with, he wrote, Moses in the laws prohibits both murder and the ritual use of blood. In any case, why should the Jews resort to homicide just to obtain blood? And if it absolutely has to be Christian blood, how do those Jews in Islamic Turkey get along? Were not the early Christians likewise charged with ritual murder? Every single alleged case of ritual murder known to date has been in fact a case of criminal murder, and the guilty parties were not Jews but Christians. In future investigations, those individuals who might stand to gain by shifting their own guilt onto the shoulders of Jews ought to be immediately suspect: feudal lords or their functionaries who have incurred financial debts; the clergy intent on providing new wonders and attractions for pilgrims; debt-ridden townsmen; witches; or parents guilty of lethal child abuse. They all have their reasons for framing the Jews as the culprits.[63]

One of the leading Hebraists of his day, Osiander was an inspired disciple of Reuchlin, and he learned to share the latter's wonderment at, and even deference to, the hidden powers and secrets of the cabala and the Talmud. This, however, did not at all entail for Osiander, any more than it did for Reuchlin, an abatement of his zeal for converting Jews. Osiander was, if anything, quite eager to rectify those Talmudic passages that had led the Jewish nation into error. In one respect, however, Osiander left his master trailing far behind, for not only did he esteem the learned rabbi, the Baruch figure of the *De verbo mirifico*, he also came to the defense of the simple Jew, that plaything of superstitious Christian imbecility.

It was precisely this feature of Osiander's program that infuriated Johannes Eck (1486–1543). A Luther adversary from the start, Eck was Germany's most notable counter-reformer. Although once Reuchlin's host in Ingolstadt (December 1519), he never shared the latter's respect for Judaic learning—to say nothing of the "common Jew." Eck now wrote a reply to Osiander, a book whose express purpose was to furnish the anti-Jewish frenzy that was rife in the streets and pubs with a scientific basis, hence, credibility. In the process, Eck succeeded in outstripping all previous Reformation publications on the theme—in crudity, spleen, and slander. The title of his work was *Against the Defense of the Jews (Ains Juden-büechlins Verlegung)*.[64]

The antecedents[65] of this pamphlet can be quickly summarized. Shortly after Easter 1540 in Tittingen (now Titting) in Middle Franconia, Jews were charged with the death of the little Michael Pisenharter. Two Jews from Sulzbach near Augsburg tried to help the accused, submitting in their defense an anonymous "opinion" written in the year 1529. The bishop of Eichstätt, who in his function as bishop simultaneously held the chancellorship of the University of Ingolstadt, handed the case on to his vice-chancellor, Johannes Eck. The latter, a seasoned counter-reformer with over twenty years battle experience, immediately caught wind of "Reformation" in the opinion and concluded that the author had to be a "Lutheran preacher." With unshakable conviction he pointed to Osiander, a man so beset with heretical blindness that he now regarded Jews to be a notch or two above Christians; he doubtless fantasized that they were Lutherans, Eck mocked.[66]

Employing against Osiander the same rhetoric that Reuchlin had used in his *Augenspiegel* to discredit Pfefferkorn as the *Tauft Jud* ("baptized Jew"), Eck now labels the Nuremberg reformer a "Jew-protector" and a "Jew-father" who has the wicked impudence to charge the authorities with greed instead of confronting the Jews with their own guilt. The Jews obviously have filled Osiander's pockets with his due share of the golden calf. The suspicion of ritual murder is well founded, since in the final analysis, the Talmud explicitly commands the Jews to kill Christian children.[67] If Osiander should now object that no baptized Jew has ever attested to anything of the kind, the appeal to Pfefferkorn proves absolutely nothing. This baptized Jew can only speak for himself.[68] And to drag into the debate Reuchlin's authority is equally inadmissible. The picture of the Jews that emerges from the "honorable doctor's" *Augenspiegel* differs from Pfefferkorn's only in a few minor details. Besides, Reuchlin himself has never denied the existence of Talmudic prayers aimed against Christians.[69]

Eck claims knowledge of a case of ritual murder from 1503 in Freiburg,[70] not to mention many other "well attested" and documented cases. Whey else were the Jews driven out of so many cities and countries? He then runs through the expulsions of the last half-century, beginning with the Spanish banishment of 1492, and bringing the record up to the present day. Hatred toward Jews is thus legitimated by reference to an unbroken tradition already centuries old. Imperturbable and unerring, the conscience of Christianity has spoken.

Eck scales the height of fury when in a single sentence he reviles the Jews no fewer than nineteen times, culminating with the scathing epithet: "a blasphemous race."[71] Quite to the astonishment of those inclined to view Luther as an opponent of the Jews, Eck does not hesitate to draw the logical conclusion of his diatribe: the "Jew-father," who is determined to whitewash the Jews, is a fledgling from the nest in Wittenberg and the most recent offshoot of Luther's line.[72] "It is the devil who speaks through you Lutherans; he would like nothing better than to acquit the Jews of their murders."[73] The correlation of Reformation and "Jewish evil" is not Eck's invention. It happens, however, that previously the two were connected the other way around. Josel von Rosheim, the first royally appointed representative of German Jewry, reported changes made at the Diet of Augsburg in 1530 to the effect that Jews had been responsible for the outbreak of the Reformation.[74] Eck now turns the tables and points to the intellectual mayhem that Luther has caused: "Luther-son" and "Jew-father" are just two sides of the same coin. Mulish insistence upon the principle of scriptural authority leads to the overvaluation of the Hebrew Old Testament[75] and to the heretical surrender to the dead letter of the Jews.

Eck is here equating the Lutheran Reformation with pro-Judaism, an equation that does not add up, at least not when Luther is taken into account. At the same time, Eck demonstrates that it is equally unthinkable to restrict a study of the roots of anti-Semitism in the age of humanism and the Reformation to Luther alone.

4

Erasmus of Rotterdam:
The Limits of Toleration

Three points are crucial to any consideration of the posture taken by Erasmus toward the Jews. The first is the fact that scholarship has not yet assimilated the results of Guido Kisch's work on Erasmus and Judaism.[76] To be sure, it is no small task to reconcile Kisch's overall conclusion, encapsulated in his remarks on the "deeply rooted, unbounded hatred for Jews held by Erasmus," with our no less deeply rooted respect for the great Dutchman's Christian humanism, his *philosophia christiana*.[77] Kisch's finding is not consistent with the sum total of energies Erasmus poured into his ideals of peace and toleration, and it ultimately compromises the plea Erasmus made for a new education that would overcome every barrier and serve as the foundation for the inalienable rights of humankind. In point of fact, however, the case against Erasmus has not been overstated.

In fact, Erasmus actually suspected the Jews (including Pfefferkorn) of collective conspiracy, and he held them culpable as the wirepullers of the Peasants' War.[78] In a letter dating from 1516 (1517?), Erasmus could note as a praiseworthy accomplishment that France is the "purest blossom of Christianity, since she alone is uninfested with heretics, Bohemian schismatics, with Jews and with half-Jewish marranos."[79] A baptized Jew never becomes a full-fledged Christian. He remains a half-Jew. The scurrilous Pfefferkorn, for that matter, is more than half a Jew: "If one were to operate on him, six hundred Jews would spring out"[80] Should someone fall from favor with Erasmus, as in the case of the papal nuntius Aleander, the explanation was readily at hand: the man must be a Jew. Nor was his wrath against Pfefferkorn directed solely *ad hominem*. The *Tauft Jud* was living confirmation of the dangers in baptizing Jews at all: we ought to be cautious about receiving Jews into the fellowship of the church.[81] In order to stem the new tide of Judaism, Erasmus was even prepared to jettison the Old Testament. In this way, the New Testament and the unity of the church could remain intact: "If only the church would not accord the Old Testament such great significance! It is a book of shadows, given on loan, until the coming of Christ."[82]

Our second observation concerns the limits of toleration and the shape they assumed in the case of Erasmus. Erasmus would have had no patience with the modern, enlightened ideal of toleration—of indivisible human rights that extend to every race and creed. What concerned him was not the freedom of the individual so much as the freedom of the individual scholar—not the risky freedom of a Christian being, such as Luther conceived it, but rather the protected free range of a Christian intellect, such as would allow him to publish the results of research unhampered by schools and their persuasions, unthreatened by church and politics. Set in this context, the apparently contradictory judgments Erasmus passed on Reuchlin within the brief span of three years become intelligible. In 1519, in the first edition of his *Colloquia* (Louvain), Erasmus flatly asserts, "I am not a Reuchlinist. I have never backed him, and he would never have wanted me to do so."[83] When, however, Reuchlin died in the summer of 1522,[84] Erasmus hastily appended his *Apotheosis Capnionis,* the assumption and beatification of Reuchlin, to his expanded, second edition of this same *Colloquia* while it was still in press at Basel. In this *in memoriam,* the deceased is venerated as a second Jerome, as the successor, in other words, to that great philologist and undaunted Bible exegete among the church fathers—for Erasmus, no doubt the highest accolade imaginable.[85]

Erasmus is far from portraying Reuchlin as a champion of Jewish erudition. He presents him instead as a sacrifice—indeed, thinly disguised as the sacrificial offering of the Jews. Exceptional intellects, he said, are never safe from Satan, and least of all today. His methods are unchanged since he moved against Jesus Christ, and his intermediaries are always scribes and Pharisees, no matter what the guise.[86] Erasmus revered in Reuchlin not the Hebraist and cabalist, but the paradigm of incorruptible fidelity to the sources, one who, like himself, had to brave the hostilities of the Dominican obscurantists.[87] Erasmus was undoubtedly an advocate of tolerance—in the face of inquisitorial animosity toward education. His tolerance was, however, of too purely an intellectual cast for him to exert a moderating influence on anti-Jewish elements. Academic freedom and Christian tolerance do not bring Erasmus to the threshold of acceptance; not, at least, where toleration and emancipation of Jews are concerned. The church critic Erasmus coined the oft-repeated phrase, "If to hate the Jews is the proof of genuine Christians, then we are all excellent Christians" (*Si christianum est odisse Iudeos, hic abunde Christiani sumus omnes*).[88] And yet this criticism and reproof of the church never became the criterion and proof of a new outlook on the Jews.

Now for the third and final consideration: the entire body of Erasmus's thought is permeated by a virulent theological anti-Judaism.[89] By this is not meant a social or political hostility to Jews, let alone racial anti-Semitism. In the course of his campaigns against religious formalism and its host of prescriptions and proscriptions, "Pharisee" and "scholastic" became synonymous for Erasmus, as did "Judaic" and "legalistic."[90] The immediate target of this anti-Judaism was not the Jews at all, but rather a fundamental, and in those days, burning topic of the Reformation: the tension between the superficial expression of religious sentiment and the inner search for truth, between lighted candles and burning hearts. Still, the matter-of-fact and ubiquitous use of the terms "pharisaic," "Judaic," and "Jewish" in polemical contexts betray the abject susceptibility of linguistic usage to customary frames of reference and experience: the "experience" in this case being that of a Christian society continually faced with the menace of an obdurate Israel. For Erasmus, this threat was posed against the most basic values: knowledge, the social order, and religion. He retaliated by advancing the causes of independent research, an educated society, and genuine devotion.

It should no longer surprise us if the trinity of peace, harmony, and learning was conceived exclusively for application to Christian society. Tolerance was a Christian virtue that did not make place in society for the "most pernicious plague and bitterest foe of the teachings of Jesus Christ,"[91] Judaism.

When Erasmus made a public profession of the fact that he was not a Reuchlinist, he obviously feared a heresy proceeding. He spoke out of fear, and even so, he spoke the truth: he was not a Reuchlinist.[92] Above all, Erasmus was concerned that with the renaissance of classical letters, paganism[93] and Judaism might emerge as the new intellectual forces of the day.[94] With the rediscovery of Hebrew,[95] the "pernicious plague" now stood threateningly close, inside.

5

"Prepare Ye the Way of the Lord"

It is no exaggeration to state that in the Middle Ages and in the early modern period the waves of religious fervor and the call for reform were disastrous in their consequences for the Jews. Three factors in the sixteenth century, so far as can be seen, were responsible for this, and their combined effect was a renewed escalation of anti-Jewish polemics.

The propaganda campaign of the pamphlet literature, which gradually intensified into a form of revolutionary agitation by the time of the so-called Peasants' War, was impelled, in constantly new variants, toward one goal: the renovation of society through the righteous justice of God. In addition to the massive complaints about the political extortion and fiscal draining of the empire by "Rome," a groundswell of criticism was rocking the more intimate regions in reaction particularly to the taxation policy of the secular authorities, which was making inroads into all aspects of life—from the property tax to the beer tax, from the devaluation of currency to the manipulation of weights and measures in the marketplace. Also belonging to this same phenomenon, and an essential feature of it, were the outcries against usury—the "adapting" of interest rates according to the emergencies of the moneylender—which can be heard in all quarters of the population, from the salons of the learned to the local wine taverns.[96] Because interest-charging was officially permitted only to Jews, and since the crown and the patriciate were amply reimbursed for their protection of Jews, protection of Jews was equated increasingly with protection of usury, and usury came to be identified with the hated tax. In inflammatory pamphlets that sought to mobilize the resentment of the masses against the financial policies of the princes and civic councils,[97] Jews invariably appeared as an insufferable threat to the public welfare.[98] "They are after our wealth and our livelihoods; they are even thirsting for the blood of our children."[99] Osiander's daring defense of the Jews was as untimely as Eck's accusations of child-murder must have been perfectly synchronized with the moods of the masses, enabling him to galvanize individual towns or whole regions into discharging their general dissatisfaction onto the Jews.

The charges of exploitation and murder, propagated to be sure not only among the lower levels of the population but among the thinking segments as well, were deeply rooted in the primordial fear that the Jews had joined forces with the apocalyptic powers. The church father Jerome had already perceived the link between the history of the Jews and the wrath of the apocalyptic incarnation of evil, the antichrist; and through his high authority he had succeeded in imprinting this concept indelibly upon the Middle Ages. At the end of the Middle Ages, reports that the antichrist had already been born and circumcised in Jerusalem begin to multiply. Simultaneously the likeness and counter-portrait of Jesus, he finds his first following among the Jews. In the horrifyingly unambiguous picture book for illiterates, *The Antichrist,* which was first published in 1480 (Strasbourg) and later often reprinted—it is typically Jews who flock around him and proclaim, "Yea, God hath come!"[100] The annihilating giants of the apocalypse, Gog and Magog, reported in Ezekiel (38—39), stand for the dreaded inundation of Christian culture by the reemergent ten lost tribes of Israel. Lest Ezekiel be construed as prophesying the invasion of the bloodthirsty infidels, that is, Mohammedans and Turks, Pfefferkorn assures us that Gog and Magog should be understood as direct allusions to the Jews, a nation already domiciled in the empire, the natural allies and spies of the infidels.[101]

The widely held assumption that this picture of the antichrist was a mere popular legend, the superstition of the common man, is untenable. This lord of the apocalypse is equally the product of the learned reading of the Bible by interpreters who were far less subject to caprice or speculation than they might appear in the present-day perspective. They understood themselves rather to be *speculatores,*[102] the sharp-sighted watchmen atop the parapets of the true Jerusalem, charged with deciphering the signs of the times in the light of the biblical prophecy.

Within a climate of anticipation, heightened by a looming end, the features of a horror-spewing antichrist appear terrifyingly imminent and demand the immediate mobilization of all Christian forces. This could trigger, as it did in Pfefferkorn's case, a massive campaign for

Jewish conversion. Conversion, however, is only the prelude to expulsion: should the strenuous efforts at eschatological mission fail, there remains for a Christianity baited into terror by the antichrist only radical self-definition—through expulsion.[103] The pamphlets of the age make vivid this commixture of anticipation, fear, and hope.

The impending judgment calls for immediate reform: "Prepare ye the way of the Lord, make his paths straight" (Matt. 3:3). As John the Baptist once summoned all to pave the way for the Lord, so must the church be directed now toward the final advent of Christ.[104] Since the preparation for the second coming of Christ can lead to revitalizing church reform only through the power of the Spirit, the old watchword of the apostle Paul in his Second Epistle to the Corinthians (3:6) takes on new explosive force: "The letter killeth, but the spirit giveth life." Although on the eve of the Reformation, Bible scholars like Reuchlin, Erasmus, or the young Luther accentuated this passage with individual shades of meaning, a reform-oriented consensus nevertheless crystallized around the apostle's word. The abuses in the church, seen as a consequence of legalism and externalization, were anathematized under the label of "Judaism": the aberrations in the medieval church, it was thought, could be traced back to a Jewish spirit and ethos.

The new outbreak of social ferment and apocalyptic tension poured oil onto the flames of a medieval anti-Jewish feeling that had never been extinguished.[105] The Pauline theology of reform managed to impart to anti-Judaism an ideological legitimacy that would survive even the temporary exhaustion of social and apocalyptic upheaval.

This new Paulinism, however, was not the cause of the conspicuous deterioration of the social and political situation of Jews in the empire. A glance at the dates of Jewish expulsions in the German empire shows that after 1520 only a handful of towns issued expulsion decrees (Prague, 1541; Kaufbeuren, 1543/1630; Schweinfurt, 1555; and Nordhausen, 1559), while in the years between 1388 (Strasbourg) and 1520 (Weissenburg), roughly ninety cities had resorted to this measure.[106] On the basis of chronology alone, then, biblical humanism's thrust for reform is exonerated as the cause of the municipal expulsion of Jews.

The sixteenth century is not, however, thereby absolved of all responsibility for the genesis of modern anti-Semitism. If humanism and Reformation, the most impressive products of Europe north of the Alps, did not lay the roots of anti-Semitism, neither did they fully seize upon the opportunities that were theirs as two critical movements of renovation. Anti-Jewish sentiment was not, like so much else, identified, stigmatized, and weeded out as "medieval." Without encountering so much as a protest, the emperor could issue a decree at the Diet in Augsburg on 4 September 1530 stating that all Jewish men had to identify themselves with a yellow badge on the coat or cap.[107] This measure should not be construed as a new harassment of Jews. Rather, it marks an unbroken extention of the medieval traditions, now adapted to the administrative demands of an empire committed to the unification of existing regional codes.

6

Luther Speaks Out

The subject of Luther and the Jews is reserved for a proper investigation in part 3. Isolated features have so polarized emotions that the total picture of Luther threatens to fade from sight.[108] At this point, however, a sketch of Luther in his relationship to Reuchlin and Erasmus must be risked if we are to set him in the context of the reforming impulse of his day. Here one immediately runs up against the initial question: Was Luther's voice always unambiguous, or was he not rather torn back and forth between hope and resignation in his biblical expectation of the Jewish conversion and in his hate-laden call for an uncompromising attack on the Jews?

In contrast to the popular opinion that has branded Luther an anti-Semite and credited him with being unequalled in that line until Hitler, in scholarship Luther has appeared, for over a century long, as a man of changing roles: he was, in turn, the Jews' friend and the Jews' foe. In 1523 Luther was actively lobbying for the elimination of obstacles to Jewish conversion. His blunt writings of the 1530s and 1540s, on the other hand, heap abuse and ignominy upon the Jews for their "obstinate blindness." This shift has not escaped modern scholarship any more than it did the Jews of Luther's time. Change, however, does not necessarily imply fundamental rethinking, and must not be taken as a sign that Luther had shifted his opinion of those Jews who wished to preserve their identity and evade the embrace of the Christian church.

On 11 June 1537, Luther politely but firmly declined an offer to exert his influence at the Saxon court of Electoral Prince Frederick on behalf of the Jews who, in line with the decree of August 1536, were obliged to leave electoral Saxony.[109] The "brotherliness" he was still urging in 1523[110] had not only proven ineffective as an inducement to conversion, but appeared to confirm the Jews more fixedly in their error. The fact that Jesus Christ was a Jew had been stressed in 1523 as a Christian self-criticism, with the papal church as the unmistakable target.[111] Now it was turned directly against the Jews: the pre-Christian anti-Jewish sentiment, Luther argues, the hatred that the Gentiles harbored against the Jews illuminates all the more radiantly the wonder of God, for these very non-Jews were prepared to accept a Jew, Jesus, as their Redeemer.[112] If even Gentiles can be made children of God, then the sons of Abraham ought no longer keep aloof—they should abandon their expectations of a Messiah. God has already become flesh and established his invisible realm; only conversion and baptism will lead to the messianic kingdom. The Jews should now, at last, halt their quest for an end to their worldwide diaspora.

Luther announced that he was planning a special study of this topic, an intention he ultimately fulfilled in the form of four works[113] on the Jews[114] written with a vehemence rivaled only by Johannes Eck's.[115] The basis of Luther's anti-Judaism was the conviction that ever since Christ's appearance on earth, the Jews have had no more future as Jews.

Erasmus had good reason to claim he was not a Reuchlinist. And so did Luther. In his written opinion on the Reuchlin controversy, probably dating from February 1514,[116] Luther declared Reuchlin's orthodoxy above all suspicion, and then grounded his own criticisms of the book burning in a rationale that was completely alien to the Christian cabalist:[117] Since the prophets themselves foresaw that the Jews would always curse and revile their lords and kings, even a first-semester theology student can see that to divert Jews from their blasphemies is tantamount to contradicting God and labeling him a liar. Therefore, the Dominican's enterprise was not simply unlawful, it was ungodly. And if converting Jews be the goal, book burning, banishment, and other superficial measures in a similar vein will be wholly futile, for God converts from within.[118] Not the "late" or the "middle," but even the "youngest" Luther known to us believed that the Jews as Jews had no future. Thus, although he was one with Reuchlin in the repudiation of brute force, their essential difference lay in Reuchlin's willingness to protect the Talmud against charges of blasphemy—even if that required laundering certain passages—while for Luther these "blasphemies" represented a God-ordained fact that no man could alter.

A further reason why Luther was no Reuchlinist was his explicit skepticism regarding the cabala.[119] His lively interest in Reuchlin's *De verbo mirifico* and his prompt reading of *De arte cabbalistica*[120] notwithstanding, Luther rejected the cabala as unscholarly and unsuitable for reliable exegesis. Only nosy idlers, *curiosi et ociosi*,[121] wish to devote themselves to this text. To Luther's mind, the Hebraic letters are indeed secretly filled with divine powers—for the superstitious. Only the tried and true Word of God, which is received through proper faith alone, possesses real efficacy.

In terms of their scholarly method, Luther and Reuchlin were worlds apart. Luther's modern, progressive training at the University of Erfurt had taught him to ascertain the exact meaning of words, the *proprietats verborum*, from their substantive context and grammatical connection. Summoned to Wittenberg as a young lecturer on the Bible, Luther remained faithful to this so-called nominalistic tradition. If he rejected the cabala as an unreliable exegetical tool, he did so for the same reasons that he later rejected the symbolic "meta-" reading of the Eucharist.[122] When a priest says in Christ's name, "This is my body," he is not recalling the remote past of the historical Jesus or alluding to the future return of the heavenly Christ; he is simply stating what *is*: the Lord is present. Propositions, and in particular biblical propositions, are not to be interpreted through some deeply buried meaning, but according to their plain grammatical context.[123] The nominalistic exegetical method explicitly repudiated on principle all word-magic. Throughout his life, Luther abided by this approach.

Luther was not a Reuchlinist any more than he was a "Lutheran." This surprising assertion requires at least a brief explanation. The counter-reformer Johannes Eck looked upon the reformer Andreas Osiander as a "Luther-son" and "Jew-father," the natural offspring of the Luther line. This thesis—in Eck's terminology, this "unmasking"—is unsustainable. Luther's prescriptions and cures may have undergone change, and significant change, but his diagnosis remained the same from the beginning: for their blasphemy, the Jews have been chastised with blindness and dispersal. They will never possess a land of their own.[124]

Osiander was, however, no isolated Nuremberger deviator from the Wittenberg party line. There is reason to presume that Melanchthon, Reuchlin's great-nephew, was just as unhappy over the harsh writings on the Jews of the late Luther as were some of the leading city reformers. Melanchthon sought to avoid a scandal when he suppressed the evidence for Osiander's having sent the erudite Jewish scholar from Venice, Elias Levita, a written statement of apology for Luther's splenetic tirades.[125]

More illuminating still was the stance of Justas Jonas (1493–

1555).[126] Luther's lifelong colleague and best man at his wedding, Jonas was entrusted with a unique charge: through his translation into Latin of Luther's German writings on the Jews, Luther's ideas would gain European diffusion. Jonas's autonomous viewpoint has probably gone unnoticed due to the simple fact that he lavished such praise and commendation on Luther's vision that we assume the Latin represents a faithful reproduction of Luther's position on the Jews. But Jonas ventures increasingly, and at critical junctures, to graft his own ideas onto the Luther text, ultimately adducing personal conclusions that approach those reached by modern exegetical practice.

In his preface to the Latin translation of a treatise Luther had written the year before, that is, in 1523,[127] Jonas's personal interpolations at this point are still much less a matter of explicit statement than of accentuation and shading. Jonas underscores the common features in the destinies of Jews and Christians, both of whom have been led astray—the Jews by Talmudic hairsplitting, and the Christians by scholastic subtleties.[128] Just as Christians will be won over to the cause of the Reformation by the recovery of the Holy Scriptures, so will the Jews see the light of truth if they but entrust themselves to the unadulterated testimony of Moses and the prophets. Christians should recognize their brethren and companions in destiny—the Jews—and include them in their prayers, "seeing that even among us, not all that purports to be Christian . . . deserves the name."[129] Even within this new perspective a traditional jibe comes into play. Jonas accuses the rabbis of deliberate deception: They have deluded the Jews into thinking that the kingdom of Abraham still exists. "Do they want us to believe that this kingdom can be found on the moon?"[130]

When in 1538 Luther spoke out against the Sabbatarians (Christians who adopted Jewish practices and in particular Jewish ritual laws),[131] it was again Jonas who translated the work into Latin. Here he introduced his own notions so emphatically that the resultant text distorts Luther's position, which has in fact hardened, presaging the vitriolics to come. Jonas does his utmost to offset Luther's exasperated disenchantment with the mission to the Jews and in the process manages to draw an entirely novel and positive picture of them. The papists now emerge as infinitely further removed from the Holy Scriptures than the most unworthy offshoot of Abraham's tribe ever was. The uncovering of the gospel "in our own day" has opened our eyes to the fact that never have greater "doctors of theology" existed than among the people of Israel in those times.[132] Reformation readings of the gospel lead to the realization that we Christians are in fact guests in the house of Abraham. Previously impious Gentiles, we are latecomers to the promise of God. Jonas is following Paul (Rom. 11:17) when he understands Christians to be the Gentiles grafted onto the "tree of Israel," united in one body with the Jews together under the single head of Jesus Christ.[133]

Jonas was in complete accord with Luther (the young and the old) in ascribing to the church the responsibility for the mission to the Jews: we owe it to them to save as many as we can, "as from a sinking ship."[134] Still, Jonas's notions of a common past and a common future are not Luther's. Not the conversion of the Jews but the summoning of the heathen is Jonas's key idea. The reception of the Gentiles into the bosom of Abraham and the subsequent fusion of the two peoples into one body, all made possible through Christ—this is the unprecedented, if un-Lutheran, attitude toward the Jews that Jonas put forward.

The difference between Jonas and Luther described here is not something read back into the sources after the fact and in the light of modern historical experience. It was, on the contrary, an explicit bone of contention between the two: On 21 December 1542, Luther wrote Jonas in Halle that, despite the latter's counsel, he was little inclined to abandon the topic himself, let alone to accommodate his view to that of Jonas.[135] Significantly, Luther neither rejected Jonas's approach as nonreformist nor condemned it as anti-Christian. The Wittenberg Reformation thus provided two distinct approaches to the Jewish question without, in the process, creating a division in its own camp. Luther never yields: conversion is the only route to salvation, but a mass conversion of the Jews is not to be expected. The promises made to Abraham do not refer literally to Abraham's blood and seed, nor is the biblical prophecy of salvation addressed to the Jews as Jews: Christians may "despair of the Jews with a clear conscience."[136] The Jews have been rejected by God. The homelessness of the Jews provides Luther with such overwhelming proof of this that he feels safe to take an oath: If it should happen that the diaspora comes to an end and the Jews are led back to Jerusalem, then we Christians will follow on their heels and ourselves "become Jews."[137]

We can summarize as follows: In the sixteenth century, the Jewish question in the empire was as virulent and pressing as ever, even after the great wave of the earlier expulsions had ebbed away. It is true that violent measures such as mass expulsions or forced conversions occurred for the most part before the turn of the century. But humanism and Reformation carried on the struggle against the Jews with their own weapons. These movements could not realize their hopes for a reconstruction of church and society without first settling their spiritual score with the Jews and with Judaism. The intensification and deepening of the ideological conflict was in fact a characteristic feature of the incipient new era. Both humanism and Reformation, soon complexly allied in several ways, together diagnosed the affliction of the age as symptomatic of its deepest disorders: reform demanded the absolute renunciation of a "Judaism" that had infiltrated into all aspects of life—the church and the monastery, the schools and the universities, the imperial free city and the episcopal see. Even where the Hebraic tradition found recognition as an educational power, as with Reuchlin, it had to be pried away from Judaism, since it could flourish only in Christian soil. For Erasmus, the tradition itself was merely useless ballast and legalistic deadweight to be jettisoned along with scholasticism.

Luther's position was unique. He placed great value on the Old Testament as the valid and manifest Word of God which does not withhold secrets even from the cabalistic magus himself. Nor did Luther have any intention of shielding the New Testament from the Old; rather, his goal was to reclaim the Scriptures in their entirety from the perversities they were suffering at the hands of the Jews, whether through rabbinical or scholastic exegesis. This was the motive that drove him to write against the Jews and "their lies" as well as against the papists "who had forgotten the Bible."

It would be a misconception to maintain that any of the three—Reuchlin, Erasmus, or Luther—entered the fray as an anti-Semite. Judaism alarmed them, and they exposed and then punished it first in their own ranks. They did not think in racial categories. And yet, if Reuchlin could subscribe to the charge of collective guilt; if Erasmus could conjure up the image of an eternal Jew, incorrigible even by means of baptism; and if Luther could forsake the buffeted race as God's disinherited people, then indeed there was no room left for the Jews as Jews. Opposition to Judaism in effect became opposition to Jews. From this point on, the image of the Jew, just as it stood, was no longer proof against conscription into the unfamiliar service of racial anti-Semitism.

Notes to Part One

1. First published with Pamphilus Gengenbach in Basel, 1521. Eberlin of Günzburg, *Der erst bundtsgnoss,* in *Johann Eberlin von Günzburg, Sämtliche Schriften,* ed. L. Enders, 3 vols. *Neudrucke deutscher Literaturwerke des XVI. und XVII. Jahrhunderts. Flugschriften aus der Reformationszeit* 11, 15, 18 (Halle, 1896–1902), 1: 3.

2. Siegfried Frey, "Das Gericht des Schwäbischen Bundes und seine Richter 1488–1534," in *Mittel und Wege früher Verfassungspolitik. Kleine Schriften* 1, ed. J. Engel (Stuttgart, 1979), 224–80; 274.

3. Cf. my *Werden und Wertung der Reformation. Vom Wegestreit zum Glaubenskampf,* 2d ed. (Tübingen, 1979), 316. English edition, *Masters of the Reformation: Rival Roads to a New Ideology,* trans. Dennis Martin (New York: Cambridge University Press, 1981), 249.

4. *Corpus Reformatorum,* vol. 1: *Philippi Melanct[h]onis Opera quae supersunt omnia,* 1, ed. C. G. Bretschneider (Halle, 1834; reprint ed., New York: Johnson Reprint, 1963), 34.

5. Lewis W. Spitz coined an epithet that is equally apt and that would have been even more welcomed by Reuchlin: "Reuchlin—a new Pythagoras," in *The Religious Renaissance of the German Humanists* (Cambridge: Harvard University Press, 1963), 61–80.

6. See his letter to John Colet of Paris, December 1504, in *Opus Epistolarum Des. Erasmi Roterodami,* ed. P. S. Allen et al., 12 vols. (New York: Oxford University Press, 1906–47 [=Allen]), 1: 405, 35–57. Cf. Michael Andrew Screech, *Ecstasy and the Praise of Folly* (London: Gerald Duckworth, 1980), 10.

7. *Weimarer Ausgabe, Abteilung Tischreden* (= *WAT*), 1. no. 1041, 525, 42–44; September–November 1532.

8. Ibid., 2. no. 2771a; cf. no. 2779a.

9. See esp. Myron P. Gilmore, "Italian Reactions to Erasmian Humanism," in *Itinerarium Italicum: The Profile of the Italian Renaissance in the Mirror of Its European Transformations, Festschrift für Paul Oskar Kristeller* on his seventieth birthday, ed. H. A. Oberman and Th. A. Brady, Jr. (Leiden: E. J. Brill, 1975), 61–115; 84.

10. See Ludwig Geiger, *Johann Reuchlin. Sein Leben und seine Werke* (Leipzig, 1871). Cf. James H. Overfield, "A New Look at the Reuchlin Affair," *Studies in Medieval and Renaissance History* 8 (1971): 165–207;

206; cf. 181. For the older literature, see esp. Gustav Kawerau, s.v. "Reuchlin," in *Realencyklopädie für protestantische Theologie und Kirche,* 3d ed. (Leipzig, 1905), 16: 680–88. For the Anglo-American specialized literature, see W. Schwarz, *Principles and Problems of Biblical Translation: Some Reformation Controversies and Their Background* (New York: Cambridge University Press, 1955), 61–91; esp. 70 n. 2.

11. *Weimarer Ausgabe, Abteilung Briefe* (=*WABr*), 1: 23, 28. Letter to Georg Spalatin from February 1514; an opinion on the Reuchlin controversy, probably based on Reuchlin's most recent publication, the *Defensio contra calumniatores suos Colonienses* (Tübingen, 1513).

12. In 1518 Luther referred to himself as Reuchlin's "successor" (*WABr* 1.268, 9f.; 14 December 1518). Max Brod, Reuchlin's most recent biographer, is one of the very few to see Luther in the context of a centuries-long Jewish persecution; he praises Reuchlin for not having been taken in by Luther's "flattering" and misleading statement (*Johannes Reuchlin und sein Kampf* [Stuttgart, 1965], 122). A reading of the letter will show, however, that by "successor" Luther means he stands next after Reuchlin on the blacklist of the "sophists." The reference is clearly not to academic inheritance; Luther was never a programmatic disciple of Reuchlin. One fleeting point of convergence between the two men has never been brought to attention: the elector Frederick of Saxony, who resolutely defended Luther against Rome (Cardinal Cajetan) and the empire. As early as 1513, Reuchlin saw in Elector Frederick a bulwark against ecclesiastical intervention: "Quo ardentius ad te Saxonesque tuos confugio . . . ut me contra quorumlibet latronum in cursus semper tuearis." The remark dates from 13 August 1513, in a cover letter to Reuchlin's translation of "The Life of Constantine the Great," found in *Johann Reuchlins Briefwechsel,* ed. L. Geiger (Stuttgart, 1875; reprint ed., Hildesheim, 1962), 190.

13. *Weimarer Ausgabe, Abteilung Werke* (=*WA*), 10: II. 329, 10; 1522.

14. See esp. *Medieval Aspects of Renaissance Learning: Three Essays by Paul Oskar Kristeller,* ed. E. P. Mahoney (Durham, N.C.: Duke University Press, 1974).

15. *In Our Image and Likeness: Humanity and Divinity in Italian Humanist Thought,* vol. 1 (London: Constable, 1970); and idem, "Erasmus, Augustine, and the Nominalists," *Archiv für Reformationsgeschichte* 67 (1976): 5–32; and idem, *The Poet as Philosopher: Petrarch and the Formation of Renaissance Consciousness* (New Haven, Conn.: Yale University Press, 1979), esp. 111.

16. J. H. Overfield, "A New Look at the Reuchlin Affair" (see n. 10 above), 206.

17. See Yosef Hayim Yerushalmi, *The Lisbon Massacre of 1506 and the Royal Image in the Shebet Yehudah* (New York: Ktav Publishing, 1976), 2.

18. Josef Benzing, *Bibliographie der Schriften Johannes Reuchlins im 15. und 16. Jahrhundert* (Bad Bocklet, 1955). Cf. Guido Kisch, *Zasius und Reuchlin. Eine rechtsgeschichtlich-vergleichende Studie zum Toleranzproblem im 16. Jahrhundert* (Konstanz, 1961), 71.

19. J. Benzing, *Bibliographie der Schriften Reuchlins,* 26.

20. Reprint (Stuttgart, 1964) of the Amerbach edition of *De verbe mirifico* (Basel, 1494), together with *De arte cabbalistica* (Hagenau, 1517). The second edition of *De verbo mirifico* appeared in the same year (1494)

published by Thomas Anshelm, the patron of the so-called Tübingen Academy. See my critique of this epithet in *Werden und Wertung der Reformation* (see n. 3 above), 19–24 =*Masters of the Reformation*, 17–22.

21. The thesis is the continuation of Pico della Mirandola's attempt to subordinate the secret sciences under theology with the aid of the cabala. See Charles Zika, "Reuchlin's *De Verbo Mirifico* and the Magic Debate of the Late Fifteenth Century," *Journal of the Warburg and Courtauld Institutes* 49 (1976): 104–38; 138.

22. *De verbo mirifico*, fol. a 2^r.

23. Reuchlin's word *resipiscentia* need not always mean "repentance." Ten years later, however, Erasmus uses the same word in his *Novum Instrumentum* as the Latin equivalent of the Greek word *metanoia* ("conversion").

24. *De verbo mirifico*, fol. b 5^v; cf. c 6^r. The uniqueness of Reuchlin's "three rings" concept makes for an interesting comparison with the three-way discussion in Cusanus, *De Pace Fidei*, written shortly after the fall of Constantinople in 1453. See the edition of his works by John P. Dolan, *Unity and Reform: Selected Writings* (Notre Dame, Ind.: University of Notre Dame Press, 1962), 195–237; cf. 185–194.

25. ". . . vos legitima sacra mutastis: ideoque frustra murmuratis, frustra deum invocatis quem non ut ipse vult colitis, sed inventionibus vestris blandientes etiam nos dei cultores livore immortali oditis . . ." (*De verbo mirifico*, fol. b 5^v).

26. "Nam Iudei clam ista tegunt et palam effere nolunt, ne nos tanto munere inparciant. Itaque in hoc scio non decipior plurimum fructus christiana religio consecuta est ex Iudeis, qui ad veritatem evangeliam conversi sunt" (Flavius Mithridates, *Sermo de Passione Domini*, ed. C. Wirszubski [Jerusalem: Israel Academy of Sciences and Humanities, 1963], 90, 7–10).

27. J. Benzing, *Bibliographie der Schriften Reuchlins*, 25. Cf. G. Kisch, *Zasius und Reuchlin*, 16–22; 19.

28. L. Geiger sees in the Tütsch missive "the principle of an indulgent toleration of the Jews" (*Reuchlin. Sein Leben*, 164). He points to the "laudable fact" that Reuchlin did not agitate for the expulsion of Jews. The same observation can be found in G. Kisch, *Zasius und Reuchlin*, 20. Against these views, there is Reuchlin's own: if the Jews, possibly even unintentionally, inflict damage on society with their usury, "essent per superiores nostros emendandi et reformandi seu expellendi . . ." (*Doctor Johannsen Reuchlins . . . Augenspiegel* [Tübingen, 1511], fol. H 2^v; reprinted in *Quellen zur Geschichte des Humanismus und der Reformation in Faksimile-Ausgaben*, vol. 5 [München, 1961]). One should keep in mind that Reuchlin's first patron and protector, Count Eberhard the Bearded (d. 24 February 1496) decreed in his testament that the Jews should be driven from his lands; this was executed in 1492. Reuchlin was a counselor to Count Eberhard and, together with Gabriel Biel, was a member of the Roman delegation summoned by the pope to confirm the founding of the university in Tübingen (1477). Count Eberhard's university charter excluded Jews from the city. For the most recent facts on Reuchlin's life, see Hansmartin Decker-Hauff, "Bausteine zur Reuchlin-Biographie," in *Johannes Reuchlin 1455–1522. Festgabe seiner Vaterstadt Pforzheim zur 500. Wiederkehr seines Geburtstages*, ed. M. Krebs (Pforzheim, [1955]), 83–

107. For more information on Eberhard's anti-Jewish policies, see Lilli Zapf, *Die Tübinger Juden. Eine Dokumentation* (Tübingen, [1974]), 15f.

29. G. Kisch, *Zasius und Reuchlin*, 20. Reuchlin strove to foster the social integration of converted Jews by enabling them to enter cloisters as Hebrew instructors. Their task was to spread the knowledge of the Hebrew language, the prerequisite to cabala study. See the revealing autobiographical letter to Ellenbogen, dating from March 1510, in Nikolaus Ellenbogen, *Briefwechsel,* ed. A. Bigelmair and F. Zoepfl, *Corpus Catholicorum* 19/21 (Münster, 1938), 54ff.

30. L. Geiger, *Reuchlins Briefwechsel,* 88f.

31. The only halfhearted support of Reuchlin by the large majority of the humanists is in fact explained by their preference for Greek and Latin, over Hebrew, authors. As Hans Widmann noted, the great Hebraist scarcely found a market for his fine grammar, *De rudimentis* ("Zu Reuchlins Rudimenta Hebraica," in *Festschrift für Josef Benzing,* ed. E. Geck and G. Pressler [Wiesbaden, 1964], 492–98). Apparently, Hebraic studies at this time were not in vogue, either in the scholastic citadels like Cologne or in the learned humanistic community.

32. L. Geiger, *Reuchlins Briefwechsel,* 93.

33. Ibid., 90.

34. "At gravius insurgent, credo, invidi contra Dictionarium nostrum in quo multorum frequenter interpretationes taxantur. Proh scelus, exclamabunt, nihil indignius patrum memoria, nihil admissum crudelius, cum ille homo audacissimus tot et tam sanctos viros divino spiritu afflatos labefactare contendat. Hieronymi beatissimi scriptura, Gelasio Papa teste, recepta est in ecclesia, venerabilis pater Nicolaus de Lyra, ordinarius expositor Bibliae, omnibus Christifidelibus vir integerrimus probatur" (ibid., 97).

35. Ibid., 98.

36. Cf. ibid., 91f.

37. Ibid., 93.

38. Ibid., 100.

39. G. Kisch, *Zasius und Reuchlin,* 23–36.

40. *Augenspiegel,* fol. E 4^v; cf. Johannes Reuchlin, *Gutachten über das jüdische Schrifttum,* ed. and trans. A. Leinz-v. Dessauer (Konstanz, 1965), 106f.

41. *Augenspiegel,* fol. J 3^r; H 2^v; see n. 28.

42. "Not all of the Talmud should be taken from the Jews and burned— only those portions which contain blasphemy should be eliminated. But only in such a way that these can at least be put into the hands of the bishops, so that they will be available to Christian Hebraists. And if Jews should continue to produce nonsensical interpretations, then our textual experts can come forth to refute and condemn them" (*Augenspiegel,* fol. F 3^r).

43. ". . . aliqui essent conservandi . . ." (*Augenspiegel,* fol. H 2^r). On this point I part company with Wilhelm Maurer, who concludes his excellent study with the following remarks: "Educational progress instead of mission to the Jews—that is basically Reuchlin's program with which he anticipates the late-eighteenth-century program of Jewish emancipation" (*Kirche und Synagoge. Motive und Formen der Auseinandersetzung der Kirche mit dem Judentum im Laufe der Geschichte* [Stuttgart, 1958], 38).

44. See G. Kisch, *Zasius und Reuchlin*, 75 n. 3.

45. Translated as *Speculum adhortationis Judaice ad Christum*. My quotations are from the Latin edition, "Editum Colonie per Iohannem pefferkorn [*sic*] olim Judeum modo Christianum. Anno domini 1507. feria tertia post Decollationem sancti Joannis baptiste."

46. Meier Spanier has questioned the authenticity of Pfefferkorn's pamphlets. The Latin works he dispenses with quickly: "He knew no Latin" ("Zur Charakteristik Johannes Pfefferkorns," *Zeitschrift für die Geschichte der Juden in Deutschland* 6 [1936]: 209–29; 210). Even in the pamphlets written in German he detects signs of outside influence. Pfefferkorn's Hebraic and Talmudic learning was supposedly lamentable: "He knew no more and no less than any other unschooled Jew of his time; as for the Talmud, he knew nothing about it" (ibid., 212). Lastly, every "archaic" German expression is for Spanier proof that someone from Cologne with "humanistic" training was responsible. The *Speculum adhortationis Judaice* (*Judenspiegel*, Latin and German editions, 1507) gets attributed exclusively to Ortwin: "The first work may well be entirely the product of Ortwin Gratius" (ibid., 221). One telling objection to Spanier's thesis is that the Latin style of the pamphlets has little in common with late-medieval "scholastic" Latin. This may have been intentional, but then the question of true authorship must still be left open. As for Pfefferkorn's state of education, he was a guest at the home of the Rabbi Meir Pfefferkorn for several years. And, finally, he must have commanded more respect than Spanier credits him with, in view of his successful mission to the sister of Emperor Maximilian. Cf. Heinrich Graetz, *Volkstümliche Geschichte der Juden*, 3 vols. (Berlin, 1923), 3: 170–220; 175, 185.

47. Salo Wittmayer Baron does not provide a broader basis of interpretation: *A Social and Religious History of the Jews*, 17 vols., 2d ed. (New York: Columbia University Press, 1952–80), vol. 13: *Inquisition, Renaissance, and Reformation*, 184–91; 186.

48. "Therefore, confiscate and burn all the books of the Talmud together with its pack of lies and fairy tales. You will be performing an act of love in relieving them of their errors and thereby steering them onto the right road. Once they have gotten this literature out of their minds, they will turn all the more swiftly and readily to the Holy Scriptures" (*Speculum adhortationis Judaice* [=*Speculum*], fol. C 4^v). Pfefferkorn makes three proposals: Usurious interest rates should be banned, for it is more profitable to be a usurious Jew than to be a poor Christian (fol. C l^r–C 2^v). Second, the Jews should be required to attend Christian sermons. This is merely a belated thanksgiving for an earlier service: without the Jews the Christians would be worshiping false idols to this very day (*adhuc adoraretis idola;* fol. C 4^r). Third, Jewish books should be confiscated and burned: *ita magnum facietis opus charitatis*, thus you will be performing a genuine act of love (fol. C 4^v).

49. *Speculum*, fol. C 4^v–D 1^r.

50. See Guido Kisch, *The Jews in Medieval Germany: A Study of Their Legal and Social Status* (Chicago: University of Chicago Press, 1949), 129ff.; 145–53.

51. The principle of law, on the basis of which Reuchlin wants to see the Jews recognized as *concives*, namely, given the legal status of "resident

aliens," had at the end of the Middle Ages largely lost its—comparatively—positive side; for the nobility and the city fathers competed with the emperor for the "protective" taxes and usually issued residence permits valid for only six years. See the documentation published by Friedrich Battenberg, "Zur Rechtsstellung der Juden am Mittelrhein in Spätmittelalter und früher Neuzeit," *Zeitschrift für historische Forschung* 6 (1979): 129–83; appendix with documents, 171–83. The development is described by Renate Overdick, *Die rechtliche und wirtschaftliche Stellung der Juden im Südwestdeutschland im 15. und 16. Jahrhundert, dargestellt an den Reichsstädten Konstanz und Esslingen und an der Markgrafschaft Baden* (Konstanz, 1965), 158–64.

52. Cf. L. Geiger, *Reuchlin. Sein Leben* (see n. 10 above), 217.

53. *Speculum,* fol. D 3ᵛ.

54. L. Geiger, *Reuchlin. Sein Leben,* 283. Cf. H. Graetz, *Volkstümliche Geschichte der Juden* (see n. 46 above), 3: 188.

55. ". . . omnino sic fore credo, quod mutatio humanarum rerum orietur et consurgit brevi in mundo, maxime in populo christiano" (*Speculum,* fol. D 4ʳ).

56. This ambivalence is an essential component of the confiscation plan itself: "Confiscation is not a violence to be perpetrated against the Jews, but is rather a means to their redemption." At the same time: "The Church will not be able to live in peace as long as these idols, these false books, are in our midst and are not destroyed" (ibid., fol. D 1ʳ).

57. By way of illustration, a passage from Luther's famous tract of 1523: "They have been misled too profoundly and for too long. As a consequence, they need to be handled clinically; for they are all too well indoctrinated in the idea that God cannot be a man. Therefore it is my plea and counsel that they be dealt with carefully, and taught from the Scripture, so that some of them might gather a few things from it. But seeing that we now handle them only with violence, and go around spreading false reports about them, charging them with taking Christian blood so that they won't stink and the devil only knows what else, and as they are considered no better than dogs—when we do all this, what good can we expect to do them? *Item,* that they are forbidden to work, trade, and to conduct other ordinary human commerce, and consequently are driven into practicing usury—how is this going to make them better? If we intend to help them, we have to practice the law not of the pope but of Christian love, and accept them benevolently, allowing them to trade and work with us, and so give them cause and opportunity to be in our midst, and to hear and see for themselves our Christian teachings. If some are stiff-necked, what difference does it make? We are surely ourselves not all good Christians" (*WA* 11: 336, 19–34).

58. See *Speculum,* fol. E eᵛ.

59. This holds right up to Luther's last sermon. Cf. *WA* 51: 195f. The same view is expressed as early as 1514: *WA* 3: 329, 26–29.

60. If Jews kill small Christian children at all, this they do out of vengefulness and not in order to get hold of their blood: "Fugite ergo et vitate orationem hanc ridiculam, falsam, et (si recte conspicere vultis) nobis christianis non parum contemptui existentem" (*Speculum,* fol. D 1ᵛ).

61. Gottfried Seebass, "Verzeichnis der Werke Andreas Osianders," *Das*

reformatorische Werk des Andreas Osiander (Nürnberg, 1967), 6–58; 17, no. 80. In the *Bibliographia Osiandrica. Bibliographie der gedruckten Schriften Andreas Osianders d.Ä.* (1496–1552), ed. G. Seebass (Nieuwkoop, 1971), this tract is furnished with the date "1540?" and the comment, "Original publication not found" (ibid., 124, no. 29). My colleague from Erlangen, Professor Gerhard Müller, kindly put into my hands a copy of the only extant edition, which belongs to a private American collection. Moritz Stern edited the text under the title, *Andreas Osianders Schrift über die Blutbeschuldigung* (Kiel, 1983).

62. Emanuel Hirsch, *Die Theologie des Andreas Osiander und ihre geschichtlichen Voraussetzungen* (Göttingen, 1919), 276–80; G. Seebass, *Das reformatorische Werk des Andreas Osiander,* 82–85. Osiander's position vis-à-vis the Jews is evident in his telling proposal of 17 February 1529, submitted to the Nuremberg city council, in which he requests permission to receive Aramaic lessons at his home from a Jewish teacher: "Now it is incontestable that the Jews understand both the Law and the prophets better than we Christians (excepting the fact that the person whom we consider to be Christ they deny), and that in other respects they have a wide understanding and know many a great secret which they do not make use of at the moment, since they no longer study, but only funnel their energies into usury and other wicked matters. It most certainly would be worthwhile for Christians to acquire such knowledge, not only for use against the Jews, but also for their own personal use. But this is impossible without an understanding of the Chaldean language. And since within the past several hundred years no Christian has been able to obtain this knowledge, unless perhaps Count Pico della Mirandola, whose death arrived all too soon, then we must learn it from the Jews; for to be self-taught in the subject is impossible, particularly when we lack the reliable basis of all philology, grammars and lexicons" (Andreas Osiander d.Ä., *Gesamtausgabe,* vol. 3: *Schriften und Briefe 1528 bis April 1530,* ed. G. Müller and G. Seebass [Gütersloh, 1979], 337, 14–25). This application may have been the occasion for rumors to the effect that Osiander was a Jew. See also G. Seebass, *Reformatorisches Werk,* 82–85.

63. "Twelfth: Baptized Jews have been slurred in various places and ways by clever erudites and wise men, and yet not a one has ever confessed that he knew anything about it or that he believed it to be true. Now not only do those Jews who know the truth by the grace of God receive baptism, but also at times those Jews who, due to their mistreatment by their fellow Jews, are despised, rejected, and banished from their own communities. Now, neither party has any cause to deny the facts if indeed these are facts. For the true believers should confess it and reveal it to the Lord Christ, in his honor, in order that the Christians be warned and a way be sought that will steer them clear of this wickedness. The rest who likewise become Christians, but out of hatred for the Jews, should not withhold this information from their enemies and persecutors. For example, in Cologne, Pfefferkorn divulged much in his testimony that told against the Jews; whether everything he said is or is not true, this is not the place to seek to prove. He did, however, have some information about child murder, which was a joy for him and his sermonizing monks to testify to and to make known to the general public" (*Ob es war*

und glaublich sey, dass die Juden der Christen kinder heymlich erwürgen
und jr blut gebrauchen ein treffenliche schrifft auff eines yeden urteil gestelt
[1529?], fol. b 1ᵛ–b 2ʳ).

64. Ingolstadt, 1541. Durch Joh. Ecken. The basis here is the 1542
edition from the library at the University of Freiburg.

65. Johann Caspar Ulrich discusses this "case" in a study which he
concludes with the words: "We close these loathesome murder stories, and
gladly admit that out of the many acts of murder with which the Jews have
previously been saddled, the greatest number are of scandalous and irre-
sponsible attribution. Nor does it redound to the honor of Christianity that
these traditional martyrs have been made into saints" (*Sammlung Jüdischer
Geschichten, welche sich mit diesem Volk in dem XIII. und folgenden
Jahrhunderten bis auf MDCCLX. in der Schweitz von Zeit zu Zeit zugetra-
gen. Zur Beleuchtung der allgemeinen Historie dieser Nation herausgegeben*
[Basel, 1768], 92; 87).

66. J. Eck, *Ains Judenbüechlins Verlegung*, fol. G 2ᵛ.

67. Ibid., fol. G 3ʳ.

68. Ibid., fol. N 4ʳ⁻ᵛ.

69. Ibid., fol. H 3ᵛ.

70. The reports Eck alludes to stem from "a congregation with a long
tradition of extraordinary anti-Jewish sentiment" (Steven W. Rowan, "Ulrich Zasius and the Baptism of Jewish Children," *Sixteenth Century Journal*
6, 2 [1975]: 3–25; 7; German Translation: "Ulrich Zasius und die Taufe
jüdischer Kinder," *Zeitschrift des Breisgauer Geschichtsvereins* ["*Schau-
ins-Land*"] 97 [1978]: 79–98; 82).

71. *Ains Judenbüechlins Verlegung*, fol. J 3ʳ.

72. "... here comes a new fruit, a Lutheristic one, that wants to doctor up
the child murders of the Jews" (ibid., fol. N 4ʳ).

73. Ibid., fol. Q 4ʳ.

74. Cf. Selma Stern, *Josel von Rosheim. Befehlshaber der Judenschaft im
Heiligen Römischen Reich Deutscher Nation* (Stuttgart, 1959), 83.

75. Why, Eck slyly continues, did not the *Confessio Augustana* (1530)
repudiate the Vulgate and build its argumentation on the basis of the
Hebrew text (*Ains Judenbüechlins Verlegung*, fol. Q 1ʳ⁻ᵛ)!

76. *Erasmus' Stellung zu Juden und Judentum* (Tübingen, 1969). In his
article "Erasmus und die Juden," *Nederlands Archief voor Kerkgeschiedenis*
60 (1980): 22–38, Cornelis Augustijn underscores, with the utmost clarity
and pertinence, that "Iudei" refers to the Christian who is more often than
not legal-minded. I cannot, however, agree with his conclusion that Erasmus
respects individual Jews "sub specie aeternitatis": "Judaism has no future as
a religion; Jews indeed do" (ibid., 37). Erasmus is not alone among his
contemporaries in his expectation that all the Jews will convert in the end.
The tragedy of this conception, namely, that of a toleration grounded in the
assumption of conversion, can be witnessed in the following capsulation by
Erasmus: "... quia Paulus praedixit fore ut Judaei tandem aggregentur ad
ovile Christi, toleramus impiam ac blaspheman gentem ..." (*Declarationes
ad censuras facultatis theologiae parisiensis, Opera omnia* [Leiden, 1703–6;
reprint ed., London, 1962], IX: col. 909AB; cited from C. Augustijn, 37 n.
95). Simon Markish offers no new insights beyond Augustijn: *Erasme et les
Juifs* (Lausanne, 1979).

77. G. Kisch, *Erasmus' Stellung zu Juden und Judentum,* 29. In the Toronto edition of Erasmus's letters, which is exemplary both in its translation and commentary, Erasmus's position vis-à-vis the Jews in connection with Pfefferkorn (here labeled a Dominican!) is characterized as an unparalleled exception (*Collected Works of Erasmus. The Correspondence of Erasmus* [=*EL*], trans. R. A. B. Mynors and D. F. S. Thomson [Toronto: University of Toronto Press, 1974ff.], 5: 164).

78. G. Kisch, *Erasmus' Stellung zu Juden und Judentum,* 37.

79. Allen (see n. 6 above), 2: 501, 10–13; *EL*, 4: 279, 12–15; 10 March 1517.

80. Allen, 3: 127, 24; *EL,* 5: 181, 29.

81. Allen, 3: 127, 37–38; *EL,* 5: 181, 42f.

82. Allen, 3: 253, 25f; cf. *EL,* 5: 347, 26–28.

83. Erasmus understandably has an interest in denying that he was a collaborator in the publication of the *Illustrorum virorum Epistulae* of 1519, particularly after Hochstraten had published the *Destructio Cabale* in April 1519, in which he also attacked Erasmus's *Novum Instrumentum.* See Allen, 4: 120–22; 121; 13: 16f. Erasmus's alibi is unreliable on two counts, since Reuchlin explicitly requested that Erasmus take up his cause (Allen, 1: 556, 22–28; *EL*, 2: 285, 25–33; April 1514), and since Erasmus had written on Reuchlin's behalf to Cardinal Riario (d. 1521), who generally was considered to be *papabilis* (Allen, 2: 73, 135–38; *EL,* 3: 91, 145–48; 15 May 1515).

84. In Bad Liebenzell on 30 June 1522. See Hans Rupprich, "Johannes Reuchlin und seine Bedeutung im europäischen Humanismus," *Johannes Reuchlin 1455–1522* (see n. 27 above), 10–13; 33. Cf. Allen, 5: 124, 46, and the corresponding note.

85. Reuchlin's name belongs in the calender of saints, just as his books belong in the libraries, ". . . proxime divum Hieronymum" (*Desiderio Erasmo da Rotterdam, L'apotheosi di Giovanni Reuchlin,* trans. G. Vallese [Naples, 1949], 130, 210f.).

86. Ibid., 134, 247–57.

87. Cf. his letter to John Fisher of 1 September 1522 (Allen, 5: 123, 19f.).

88. To Hochstraten, 11 August 1519 (Allen, 4: 46, 142f.).

89. The corresponding phenomenon in Jerome, for Erasmus *the* exegete among the Fathers, is elucidated in Horst Dieter Rauh's *Das Bild des Antichrist im Mittelalter: Von Tyconius zum Deutschen Symbolismus,* 2d ed. (Münster, 1979), 132f.

90. Especially precise formulations in *Commentarii in Psalmum "Beatus vir"* [Psalm 1] *finis,* appended to the second edition of *Enchiridion* (Basel, 1518). See Erasmus, *Opera omnia* (as in n. 75), V: col. 182B.

91. To Capito, 26 February 1517 (Allen, 2: 491, 138f.; *EL,* 4: 267, 154f.).

92. See Charles Zika, "Reuchlin and Erasmus: Humanism and Occult Philosophy," *Journal of Religious History* 9 (1977): 223–45; 229.

93. ". . . caput erigere conetur paganismus" (Allen, 2: 491, 135).

94. "Nunc audimus apud Bohemos exoriri novum Judaeorum genus, Sabbatarios appellant, . . ." *De amabili* [Allen: *Liber de sarcienda*] *Ecclesiae concordia,* with a dedication to Julius Pflug, from 31 July 1522 (Erasmus, *Opera omnia,* V: col. 505D–506A). Cf. "Dicuntur et hodie repullulascere

Sabbatarii, qui septimi diei otium incredibili superstitione observant,"
Ecclesiastae, sive de ratione concionandi, Book III with dedication to Christoph von Stadion, 6 August 1535 (ibid., col. 1038B).

95. ". . . ne renascentibus Hebraeorum literis Iudaismus meditetur per occasionem reviviscere" (Allen, 2: 491, 137f.).

96. See my discussion in *Werden und Wertung der Reformation,* 263–66. =*Masters of the Reformation,* 130ff.

97. Cf. Johannes Teuschlein, "Solution to Several Questions in Praise and Honor of Jesus Christ and His Mother Mary Against the Obstinate Blind Jews and All Those Who Maintain Them Illegally in Their Lands and Locations, Let Them Travel, and Otherwise Make Indulgent Concessions, As Is Newly the Case," printed by Fryderich Peypus (Nuremberg, 1520).

98. "Since it is the case that as things now stand in the world, generally all the estates are burdened with this diabolical avarice, there is more utility for us in ridding ourselves of the Jews than in tolerating them" (Teuschlein, fol. C 2^r). "Since the Jews inflict so much harm on our bodies and souls, worth and property, the law of nature teaches us that we should expel them as best we can" (fol. C 3^r). "If, on the other hand, we look at the conduct of spiritual and secular men, we find that they have so sated themselves to the limit on the Jews' property that one can hardly pry the booty from their maws; and thus are the Jews only with difficulty driven from such places as they occupy" (fol. C 4^v). Mary in answer to a prayer: "You ask me for this; so enact my will, and drive away from yourself that great enemy of mine and of my dear son" (fol. C 5^r).

99. In an anonymous pamphlet, the accusation of ritual murder is denied, not to defend Jews but to aggravate even further the charge: they do not need Christian blood for "medicinal" purposes, but only to appease their savage vengefulness: "What I have to say is credible, for their entire Easter Day is only designated so that their enemy will confront them on earth, face to face, just as the Pharaoh, who formerly was their lord, drowned in the sea with his whole people; and since today there are no more Pharaohs, they take a Christian lad and pour out his blood as one enemy does to another." *Disgrace and effrontery done by the Jews to the image of Mary, which had been commissioned by Maximilian the Holy Roman Emperor as a lasting monument in the praiseworthy city of Cologne, from which they have also been eternally banished,* s.a.s.l. [Thomas Murner (?), Strasbourg, 1515], fol. D 5^r. "I am given to understand what has happened in the Spanish lands where Jews determined among themselves, and set it down in a concilium, that as far as possible no Jew would pass an Easter Day without Christian blood; this would be a sign for all who were present and eating their hand-made matzos, that this was Christian blood, and we their eternal enemies" (fol. D 6^v). "Thereby they confirmed their brotherhood in the powers of such blood. The Christian has indeed no greater enemy than the Jew. They crave our blood daily, in order that they should be our masters; they thirst every hour and minute after our blood—true bloodhounds. Therefore we should treat them in a commensurate way, seeing how they chose to remain such rogues as they are. We have drawn into our midst a snake whose poison is sheer death, without antidote, and constantly multiplying against Christianity and the Lord our Father" (fol. E 1^r).

100. *Der Antichrist und Die Fünfzehn Zeichen vor dem Jüngsten*

Gericht. Faksimile der ersten typographischen Ausgabe eines unbekannten Strassburger Druckers, um 1480, 2 vols. (text and commentary), ed. Ch. P. Burger et al. (Hamburg, 1979), Text volume 5.2; cf. esp. the commentary of Christoph Peter Burger, "Endzeiterwartung im späten Mittelalter. Der Bildertext zum Antichrist und den Fünfzehn Zeichen vor dem Jüngsten Gericht in der frühesten Druckausgabe," Commentary volume 18–53; 36, 39, 43.

    101. Ibid., 47ff.

    102. See my discussion in "Fourteenth-Century Religious Thought: A Premature Profile," *Speculum* 53 (1978), 80–93; 90f. For abundant material, see Hans Preuss, *Die Vorstellungen vom Antichrist im späten Mittelalter, bei Luther und in der konfessionellen Polemik. Ein Beitrag zur Theologie Luthers und zur Geschichte der christlichen Frömmigkeit* (Leipzig, 1906), 12ff., and Joshua Trachtenberg, *The Devil and the Jews: The Medieval Conception of the Jew and Its Relation to Modern Antisemitism* (New Haven: Yale University Press, 1943; New York: Oxford University Press, 1966), 32–43.

    103. George, Duke of Bavaria (1486–1529) and Bishop of Speyer (1515–29), bases his argumentation on the concept of God's wrath in a previously overlooked and blunt "mandate" from 4 April 1519 against the Jews who "are more akin to dogs than to human beings." As in Pfefferkorn, so here too we find the excuse that the authorities have been corrupted by the Jews: "Quocirca officii nostri esse visum est tante hominum seu potius canum perversitati quocumquemodo resistere aut obviam ire, et eo magis cum seculares prefecti quorum esset [officium] hec nephanda ob christi gloriam prohibere, non solum hec non prohibeant, sed interdum (judeorum donis corrupti) etiam tolerent et quantum in ipsis est non sine gravi peccato tutentur. ... Cum autem verendum sit ne divinam propter hoc indignationem incurramus ... pro contumeliam creatoris respublica ledatur, fames, terremotus et pestilentia (qua etiam nunc laboratur) fiat, dum nimis paciente christi dei nostri opprobria sustinemus. ... Volumus ... sub excommunicationis pena publice moneatis et requiratis ne posthac judeis cohabitent sive cum eis manducent neque servitia aliqua illis prestere aut proles eorum mercede lactare vel nutrire aut medicinam ab eis recipere presumant aut frequentiorem cum eis conversationem habeant ..." (*Mandat gegen die Juden* [Hagenau, Heinrich Gran, 1519], university library, Tübingen; call no.: Gb 599.2°).

    104. See my typology in *Forerunners of the Reformation: The Shape of Late Medieval Thought* (New York: Holt, Rinehart & Winston, 1966; Philadelphia: Fortress Press, 1981), 4–14.

    105. Cf. Peter Herde, "Probleme der christlich-jüdischen Beziehungen in Mainfranken im Mittelalter," *Würzburger Diözesan-Geschichtsblätter* 40 (1978): 79–94; esp. 88.

    106. See the "table of expulsions" compiled by Philip N. Bebb in "Jewish Policy in Sixteenth Century Nürnberg," *Occasional Papers of the American Society for Reformation Research* 1 (1977): 125–36; 132f. Bebb emphasizes that his figures are only approximations. For a complementary set of figures, for example, including the Donauwörth expulsion of 1517, see Helmut Veitshans, *Die Judensiedlungen der schwäbischen Reichsstädte und der württembergischen Landstädte im Mittelalter,* in *Arbeiten zum historischen Atlas von Südwestdeutschland* 5 (Stuttgart, 1970), 12–43; 38.

107. "Also the Jews shall carry a yellow badge on their coat or cap, prominently and at all times, toward their identification in public" (*Urkundenbuch zu der Geschichte des Reichstages zu Augsburg im Jahre 1530,* ed. K. E. Förstemann, vol. 2: *Von der Übergabe der Augsburgischen Confession bis zu dem Schlusse des Reichstages* [Halle, 1835; reprint ed., Osnabrück, 1966], 347). More on the continuous efforts to implement such identification measures in Strasbourg and Regensburg can be found in Haim Hillel Ben-Sasson, "Jewish-Christian Disputation in the Setting of Humanism and Reformation in the German Empire," *Harvard Theological Review* 59 (1966), 369–90; 372f. On 15 October 1530, Charles V in Augsburg reconfirmed the "privileges" of Württemberg, which were "unburdened" by protective rights for Jews. This all-revealing mandate, which is cited in the literature as the "imperial charter of freedom," was edited by August Ludwig Reyscher, *Vollständig historisch und kritisch bearbeitete Sammlung der württembergischen Gesetze,* vol. IV (Tübingen, 1831), 60–65.

108. For the state of current scholarship, see esp. the comprehensive account in Johannes Brosseder, *Luthers Stellung zu den Juden im Spiegel seiner Interpreten. Interpretation und Rezeption von Luthers Schriften und Äusserungen zum Judentum im 19. und 20. Jahrhundert vor allem im deutschsprachigen Raum* (München, 1972). More recent results are assembled in C. Bernd Sucher, *Luthers Stellung zu den Juden. Eine Interpretation aus germanistischer Sicht* (Nieuwkoop, 1977). As yet unsurpassed, and probably unsurpassable, is Reinhold Lewin's analysis, *Luthers Stellung zu den Juden. Ein Beitrag zur Geschichte der Juden in Deutschland während des Reformationszeitalters,* in *Neue Studien zur Geschichte der Theologie und der Kirche* 10 (Berlin, 1911; reprint ed., Aalen, 1973). Special recognition is due Rabbi Lewin for his remarkable impartiality, which earned him the *Jahrespreis* award of the Protestant faculty of the University of Breslau. Together with his family he fell prey to the Nazi terror, after "the American embassy turned down his request for an immigration visa" (See Guido Kisch, "Necrologue Reinhold Lewin, 1888–1942," *Historia Judaica* 8 [1946]: 217–19; 219).

109. *WABr* 8: 89–91. R. Lewin, *Luthers Stellung zu den Juden,* 62ff.; S. Stern, *Josel von Rosheim* (see n. 73 above), 125–30; 137f.

110. Cf. *Jesus Christ Was Born a Jew* (1523), *WA* 11: 314–36; 315, 14–24; 336, 22–37.

111. See the material quoted in full in n. 57 above.

112. *WABr* 8: 90, 21–28; already mentioned in 1523 as one among several arguments; *WA* 11: 331, 3–8.

113. *Wider die Sabbather an einen guten Freund* (1538), *WA* 50: 312–37; *Von den Juden und ihren Lügen* (1543), *WA* 53: 417–552; *Vom Schem Hamphoras und vom Geschlecht Christi* (1543), *WA* 53: 579–648; *Von den letzten Worten Davids* (1543), *WA* 54: 28–100. The Saxon policy toward the Jews is illuminated by a promulgation by Elector John Frederick, from the year 1543, and confirmed by the mandate of 1536. This *Ausschreiben* was published at the end of the previous century by Carl August Hugo Burkhardt, "Die Judenverfolgung im Kurfürstentum Sachsen," *Theologische Studien und Kritiken* 70 (1897), 593–98; 597.

114. But see also the summary in *WA* 42: 448, 25–42; 451, 1–34. It is in the Genesis commentary (1535–45), even more than in the writings ex-

plicitly devoted to the Jews, that we find his arsenal of arguments against the Jews fully stockpiled.

115. Cf. the harsh judgment of Peter Maser, "Luthers Schriftauslegung im Traktat 'Von den Juden und ihren Lügen' (1543). Ein Beitrag zum 'christologischen Antisemitismus' des Reformators," *Judaica* 29 (1973): 71–84, 149–67.

116. *WABr* 1:23f. In Luther's first letter to Frederick's private counselor, Georg Spalatin. Cf. Irmgard Höss, *Georg Spalatin 1484–1545. Ein Leben in der Zeit des Humanismus und der Reformation* (Weimar, 1956), 75–78.

117. We have passed over Luther's first remark: Although the abuses within the church cry out for punishment, the Dominicans go knocking at the wrong doors. This is a theme that recurs in 1523 (*WABr* 1: 23, 20–30).

118. Ibid., 23, 39–42.

119. For a detailed and convincing treatment of Luther's other position on the cabala, see Siegfried Raeder, *Grammatica Theologica. Studien zu Luthers Operationes in Psalmos* (Tübingen, 1977), 59–80.

120. *WABr* 1: 149, 11—150; 14f.; February 1518.

121. *WA* 5: 384, 12; citation from S. Raeder, *Grammatica Theologica,* 79.

122. Cf. *Werden und Wertung* (see n. 3), 368ff. = *Masters of the Reformation,* 287ff.

123. Cf. *Werden und Wertung,* 208f., 224 = *Masters of the Reformation,* 163ff., 177.

124. On the Diaspora of the Jews as the visible proof of the wrath of God, see the commentary to Gen. 12:3; *WA* 42: 448, 25—451, 34; esp. 448, 34ff.

125. April 1545; see G. Seebass, *Das reformatorische Werk des Andreas Osiander* (see n. 60), 82; cf. *Corpus Reformatorum,* vol. 5: *Philippi Melanct[h]onis Opera quae supersunt omnia,* ed. C. G. Bretschneider (Halle, 1838; reprint ed., New York, 1963), 728f.

126. See also Walter Delius, *Lehre und Leben: Justus Jonas 1493–1555* (Gütersloh,1952). Jonas's letters are only partially available, in *Der Brief-wechsel des Justus Jonas,* ed. G. Kawerau, 2 vols. (Halle, 1884/85; reprint ed., Hildesheim, 1964).

127. *Libellus Martini Lutheri, Christum Ieum [sic] verum Iudaeum et semen esse Abrahae, è Germanico versus, per I. Ionam* (Wittenberg, 1524); cf. *WA* 11: 309f.

128. Jonas appended to his Latin translation a dedicatory letter in which he states that the Jews had to distance themselves from the distortions of the Talmud as much "as we should distance ourselves from the Scotist and Thomistic nonsense": "Videmus plane contigesse Iudaeis, ut haud aliter a verbo Dei et simplicitate scripturae avocati sint Thalmudicis nugis ac nos Scotisticis et Thomisticis somniis" (*Briefwechsel des Justus Jonas,* 1: 93, 4–6).

129. "Sed orandum est nobis pro hac gente, praesertim cum inter nos quoque non omnes Christiani sunt, qui titulum Christianismi gerunt" (ibid., 93, 12–14).

130. "Quin in lunares urbes regnum Iudaeorum translatum comminis-cuntur?" (ibid., 93, 11f.).

131. *WA* 50: 312–37.

132. "Nos autem, quibus Deus hoc seculo aperuit libros sacros, quibus contigit hoc tempore aspicere claram lucem evangelii, iam cognitum habemus, nullos unquam doctores theologiae verae praestantiores sub sole vixisse, quam in illo populo Israel, . . ." (*Briefwechsel des Justus Jonas* 1: 323, 19–22).

133. "We Gentiles are guests and strangers in the house of the Lord, and partake of such great gifts and blessings in Jesus Christ, the true Messiah. Formerly god-less in this world, today we are shareholders in the secrets of God, and are gathered together with Abraham and the great patriarchs into one body under the single head of Christ" (ibid., 323, 26–30; Rom. 11:25–32).

134. "Ideo cum tam nobilis et sanctus populus sunt Iudaei, ex quorum plenitudine nos omnes accepimus, profecto perpetuam nos gentes eis debemus gratitudinem, ut quantum omnino fieri potest, quosdam ex eis adhuc quasi e medio naufragio servemus" (ibid., 324, 7–10).

135. "Hactenus in Iudeorum me mersi furias, postquam tu quiescendum esse consuluisti, dum aliam viam tentaretis" (*WABr* 10: 226, 19–21). Jonas's exhausting efforts in March 1543 to translate Luther's treatise, *On the Jews and Their Lies,* are made clear in *WA* 53: 414. I doubt that the editor J. Luther is correct in his supposition that Jonas left *Vom Schem Hamphoras* untranslated due to linguistic difficulties (*WA* 53: 573).

136. "In brief: Because you see that after fifteen hundred years of misery (when no end is certain or will ever be so) the Jews are not disheartened nor are they even cognizant of their plight, you might with a good conscience despair of them. For it is impossible that God should let his people (if they were that) wait so long without consolation and prophecy" (*WA* 50: 336, 1–6).

137. "Or if such an event fails to come about, then let them head for Jerusalem, build temples, set up priesthoods, principalities, Moses with his laws, and in other words themselves become Jews again and take the land into their possession. For when this happens, they will see us come quickly on their heels and likewise become Jews. But if not, then it is entirely ludicrous that they should want to persuade us into accepting their degenerate laws, which are surely by now after fifteen hundred years of decay no longer laws at all. And should we believe what they themselves do not and cannot believe, as long as they do not have Jerusalem and the land of Israel?" (*WA* 50: 323, 36—324, 8).

For the first version of Part One, with a more exhaustive scholarly apparatus, see my "Three Sixteenth-Century Attitudes to Judaism: Reuchlin—Erasmus—Luther," in Bernard Cooperman's *Jewish Thought in the Sixteenth Century* (Cambridge: Harvard University Press, 1982).

FROM AGITATION TO
REFORMATION

The Spirit of the Times
Reflected in the "Jews' Mirror"

I am a little booklet,
the Confession of Jews by name.
I'm easily found in every town,
and want more new readers,
to be better known,
and to spread into every other land.
Whoever reads me, I wish him well,
so long as I don't fall into Jewish hands.

Johannes Pfefferkorn
Der Juden Beicht
Cologne, 1508

7

Overcoming History, Falsifying History

The earlier, more general surveys of the Reformation treat the Jewish question only in passing, while the more recent ones neglect it entirely. Such studies are designed to highlight the basic structure of a period, not to wander off into the side stages. The silence, therefore, may not even seem to represent a failing in need of correction. The age of humanism and Reformation had not yet fully outgrown the Middle Ages and was at best marginally preoccupied with the Jewish issue; to scrutinize that age for the first signs of anti-Semitism would appear misleading. What is more, the history of anti-Semitism hardly begins with the sixteenth century.[1] The historian who believes in statistics would be impressed with the additional fact that only a fraction of the early publications directly address the subject matter of "the Jews." In short, it is not surprising that the question has been relegated by and large to specialists as a separate problem without any substantive connection to the big issues of the age: the battles surrounding faith and theology, church and society, *Kaiser* and *Reich*.

The sixteenth century takes on an altogether different shape once one is prepared to look behind the course of history, behind the dates and events, and into the motives and rationales, the hopes and fears. Compilations of statistics are inadequate guides to a grasp of mindsets, and our sources reveal more than their mere quantity would lead one to think.[2] Precisely in connection with the Jewish question there arise disputes, difficulties, and emotions that expose fundamental tensions of the age. The writings on the Jewish issue, then readily adduced as a "mirror of the Jews," function for us today as a mirror of the times. And what the mirror shows us is that we cannot comprehend the scope of sixteenth-century hatred of Jews by divorcing it from the history of the period. The publications of the late Middle Ages and early Reformation, above all the pamphlets,[3] attest to the way in which the Jewish problem fermented in the confused brew of the age and surfaced in various forms.

An excellent and academically important literature specifically devoted to the history of the Jews can be found under the rubric of "Jews in the Middle Ages" or "Jews in Germany." A narrow focus on the history of the Jewish people, however, seen through the additive, cumulative lens of the chronicler and without regard for the surrounding historical circumstances, provides only another reflection of the medieval "Jews' Mirror," a reversed image appraised under somewhat more sophisticated criteria.

The following pages differ from these compartmentalized descriptions of the Jewish people's history in particular lands, territories, or cities. Here the Jewish question and its expression in early publications are approached as the mirror of an epoch, and are deliberately enlisted in the service of a history of ideas that does not sever thoughts and attitudes from the concrete aspects of life that condition them. Our hope is to detect, in the initial foundational stages of a new era, radical changes in the conditions that surround the Jewish question as well.[4]

Such lofty considerations never get beyond theory when they collide with the "poisoned well" syndrome of current historical literature—the falsification of a past in the attempt to come to grips with it in the present. Our present-day grappling with that past has forced us to realize how ticklish an undertaking it is to think through the often unmentioned Holocaust dimension: to face it straight on, without contriving to define the outcome as German history's particular, predetermined, and inevitable end. The decisive consideration is whether one succeeds in writing a history conscientious about its sources, not its guilt. There exists no worse history than where a guilty conscience guides the pen.

So we must approach with caution the names which no history of anti-Semitism omits: Pfefferkorn, this time as an agitator; Luther, no longer in the context of the elite and erudite, but as the author of lowbrow pamphlets written in the popular idiom; and lastly, the city of Regensburg as the stage on which the agitation for reform and hatred of Jews make their joint appearance.

8

The Unknown Pfefferkorn:
Outsider and Voice of His Age

In the period between 1507 and 1521, Johannes Pfefferkorn composed more pamphlets on Jews than any other individual author. Nearly all of these works were reprinted several times over in Latin or German editions, first in Cologne and soon after in Speyer, Augsburg, and Nuremberg.[5] It is hardly surprising that not even a single monograph has been devoted specifically to this alleged hater of Jews, Pfefferkorn: his writings lie tucked away, scattered in our libraries, virtually unread.

Decried as a fanatic, Pfefferkorn crops up for a brief moment as the catalyst of the controversy between the "Obscure Men" and as the trigger to the perpetually exaggerated "great offensive" of German humanism against medieval scholasticism. Not Johannes Pfefferkorn but rather his opponent and victim of the inquisition, Johannes Reuchlin, has gained general attention.[6] The first German to master all three languages necessary for Bible study, this *doctor trilinguis* acquired, as mentioned earlier, the historiographical reputation of a Jewish sympathizer battling for a new educational program against unenlightened obscurantism.

While in recent years Reuchlin has become the object of much rereading and has come to prominence in Renaissance studies as a champion both of the cabala and of "white magic," Pfefferkorn has remained shrouded in silence. The notorious passage in his first work, the *Judenspiegel* ("Jews' Mirror") of 1507, in which he formulated his demand for the confiscation and burning of the Talmudic books, has inspired no one to explore this manifest Jew-baiter, let alone his critique of the Christian establishment. By the same token, however, the connection between millenary expectation, hope of reform, church criticism, and social protest has been left virtually unnoticed.

Already in his *Judenspiegel* Pfefferkorn foresaw imminent revolution, if not the Day of Judgment itself. The conversion of all Jews had to be completed before the final reckoning. Pfefferkorn himself did not isolate the subject of the Jews but set it squarely in the contemporary context of the fear-laden pressures for reform: "Right" has to be vindicated by all available means, and as swiftly as possible. It is dangerous for the church to propagate this nonsense about Jewish ritual murders, which only puts the church in a ludicrous light and damages its own credibility. Finally, he charges, the Jewish policies of the secular authorities are determined by financial greed,[7] a theme that reverberates throughout the pamphlets until 1525, and with increasing vehemence.

"Revolution," "Judgment Day," and "indictments against church and authority" are so deeply bound up in the Jewish question that there can be no treatment of the Jewish problem that does not simultaneously reveal weak spots in the church and in society as a whole.

Pfefferkorn's pamphlets cannot be restricted to their role in the "learned controversy" of the "Obscure Men" or to the Inquisition. As is generally true of the writings against the Jews, Pfefferkorn's literary output is inflammatory, aimed at influencing the world beyond the ivory tower. His obstreperous activities thus belong to the history of civic unrest and to the early phase of the Peasants' War. The exertions of this converted Jew on behalf of his blood brethren are directed first of all at their conversion and baptism, but next at their assimilation into a society in need of reform. Pfefferkorn thus affords us a glimpse into reformist ideals, into social strains, into criticism of the age and of the church, and even into the basic components of human existence: fear, rage, and hope. Pamphlets, low-priced, often illustrated and always readable, were here the instrument best suited for informing, alarming, and mobilizing the populace.

Characteristically enough, the learned Reuchlin first discovered in 1511 that he had deprived himself of broader influence by casting his writings in a demanding Latin. If he were to instruct the public— which for him still meant the elite public, the decision-making bodies in the cities and in the territories—he had to imitate Pfefferkorn's example and impart his lessons in German. Scholarship has continually lamented the fact that Reuchlin in his *Augenspiegel* stooped to meddle in a debate with Pfefferkorn. It must indeed have been a weighty decision for the humanist to answer German and, worse yet, *such* German with German. He was moved to do so not only by the damage to his reputation in the German public eye, but also by the "baptized Jew's" teaching "that the subjects in the empire ought to plot uproar and uprising against their masters. . . ."[8] The learned Stuttgart magistrate was not simply a humanist waging solitary battle against an army of scholastics, and he was assuredly not a philo-Semite repulsing Jew-baiters. He was essentially a spokesman for the loyal, higher bourgeoisie and had detected in Pfefferkorn's pamphlets (which for Reuchlin belonged in any case to an inferior, subliterary genre) a rebelliousness that imperiled the tranquillity and order of the empire.

To repeat: the Jewish question cannot be isolated from the social reshuffling that occurred at the beginning of the sixteenth century. The seeds of open, societal discontent were not sown exclusively by Pfefferkorn and his circle. Social critique and religious tension, intermeshed and widespread throughout the cities, especially those of southern Germany, were sustained by a diverse coalition that included mendicant friars and handworkers, lower clerics and guilds. The new perspective on Pfefferkorn yields more than a revision of the prevailing assessment of an individual figure. Now another side of the Jewish question has been brought to light, a side that too easily has been obscured by the habitual association of Pfefferkorn with ruthless inquisition, scholastic ignorance, and the all-consuming hatred of a convert. The unknown Pfefferkorn is an absolute outsider and simultaneously the voice of his age. As a baptized Jew, his conversion represents to the one side a treacherous betrayal, to the other a cunning pretense. From his irremediable position of an outsider suspended between religions, he discovers the flaws on both sides: the obstinacy of the Jews, and the obtuse severity of the Christians.

As the voice of his age, Pfefferkorn provides an index of the potential for social ferment in his day, and attests to the general heightening of social strains and religious conflicts in the face of fears of the end and hopes for a new beginning. In this regard, Pfefferkorn is anything but an "outsider."

9

Luther
and the *Zeitgeist*

The fast-growing literature on Luther and the Jews[9] has been shaped extensively by the historical developments of our century. This also explains the current absorption of scholarly energies with the question of Luther's supposed reversal in 1523, the year he is to have turned his back on the Jews. With whatever intentions, Luther has been detached from his age and studied as a timeless, self-standing topic. Under these circumstances, it becomes possible, or rather, it is only logical that critics bill Luther as the chief culprit in the dramatic events of later history. Equally understandable is the position taken by those who see in the great reformer of the sixteenth century both the renovator of the Western church and the forerunner—even the "fore-thinker"—of the modern age. Luther clearly must also stand as the principal vanquisher of medieval hatred for the Jews. And indeed, Luther did make statements in 1523 that indict an entire period for its hatred of the Jews: "For they have treated the Jews as if they were dogs and not human beings."[10]

If Luther is to be identified without qualification as the early spokesman of the modern era, then it is consistent to take this statement, excerpted from his tract *Jesus Christ Was Born a Jew*, as the definitive word of the reformer who in so many areas paved new exits from the Middle Ages. But the consonance of Luther's later writings, above all the writings of the 1540s, with his written opinion on the Jews, which dates from 1514, reveals that "salvaging operations" are here underway.

Even if the discussion surrounding Luther's alleged change of heart could be resolved more swiftly than the relevant literature leads one to expect, the question of "Luther and the Jews" would still lead to a twofold dead end.

First of all, the Jews do not appear as an independent, autonomous theme in Luther's theology. From Luther's point of view, there was no such subject as "Luther and the Jews." One must look instead to the already traditional catalogue of calamities to which Luther resorted for identifying the perils of his time: the opponents of God always converge—Jews, heretics, pope, and the Turks.[11] It was not only against the Jews, but also against the Turks and heretics that Luther demanded from the authorities a tougher policy, especially in the 1530s.

A further reduction characteristic of previous Luther scholarship indicates the field's limitations. Our current expositions of the sixteenth century are as self-assured as they are uninformed, lacking all feel for the language of the coarse, popular German literature of that age and its nuances, and all sense of proportion for evaluating levels of harshness in anti-Jewish accusations. A fair evaluation of "Luther and the Jews" cannot be achieved without thorough study of his contemporaries' views on the subject. Moreover, if we are to measure the evangelical innovations of Luther's Jewish program during the years up to and including the 1540s, it is imperative that we listen to the voices of his opponents from the orthodox camp. The oldest and most unrelenting among these was the most significant counter-reformer of Germany, Johannes Eck, professor at the University of Ingolstadt. From his 1541 pamphlet, *Against the Defense of the Jews* (*Ains Judenbüechlins Verlegung*), two facts emerge. First, Eck and Luther, who were opposed on all fundamental articles of faith, are by modern standards equally merciless in their rejection of the Jews. Second, however crude and perhaps even "pure Aryan" as the title of Luther's *On the Jews and their Lies* (1543) may seem, comparison with Eck's adamant recapitulation of the medieval charges of child murder makes clear that Luther is pursuing the true, objectifiable, and essentially debatable interpretation of the Holy Scriptures. Not desecration of the host, and not Jewish bloodthirstiness, but rather theological misguidedness is what Luther attacks as life-threatening. Luther knew well what horror stories were circulating about the Jews, and believed—no doubt correctly, for anything else would be incomprehensible—that the Jews were filled with hatred for the Christians. In response, he called out for a "severe (!) mercy." For all its severity, there is indeed mercy in Luther's position, from which is banned the logic of collective guilt, and so too all justification for taking vengeance on individual Jews. Despite the shared intractability of their stances, we find that it was Luther, not Eck, who risked the leap from character assassination to the battle for truth.

Eck's Counter-Reformation propaganda portrayed Wittenberg as a hotbed of Jewish sympathy.[12] Luther's "sympathetic" work of 1523 may well have served as supporting evidence for this "exposé." Even a sympathetic posture on the Jews, however, must be observed in its proper context. For our evaluation we will call upon an earlier confederate of Luther and a yardstick of the time, Johannes Eberlin of Günzburg, the voice of the Reformation in southern Germany. Eberlin's anonymous pamphlet *The Bell Tower* appeared in 1523 in Tübingen.[13] Defying a city council ordinance, certain inhabitants from Günzburg had "run off" to attend the sermons of the evangelical pastor Hans Wehe in nearby Leipzig. For this they were punished with imprisonment and confined to the tower of the Günzburg church. Against such an abuse of the church as an instrument of injustice, Eberlin had the bell tower itself sound the alarm.

As was true in the case of Pfefferkorn here too the Jewish question was imbedded in a context of protest and expectation, wedged between a critique of social injustice and the hope of major revolution—that "alteration" which, on the basis of his observations of the heavenly constellations, the famous astrologer from Tübingen, Johannes Stöffler (d. 1531), predicted would occur in the year 1524.[14] Unlike Pfefferkorn, however, Eberlin perceives radical change not in the great revolution, but in the breakthrough of the gospel. Time, he optimistically trusts, is "mistress of truth."[15] For yet a little while the "big wigs" would continue to hold the reins of power,[16] suppress the gospel, and defy the most recent summons of the imperial Diet of Nuremburg (6 March 1523) which—on Eberlin's interpretation—restored full freedom to reformational preaching.[17] Even prisons were impotent to prevent the outburst of truth, for if towers could compel faith, why were not the Jews locked up long ago?

In the answer Eberlin himself gives, the traditional anti-Semitic charge of financial exploitation is turned on its head: exploitation is a fate that has been *inflicted* on the Jews. It is through the avarice of the unchristian, if not diabolical, authorities that Jews are driven to usury. If they are permitted to roam at large, this is only because the authorities would otherwise forfeit the ungodly tax they levy annually on the Jews, which in turn leaves the Jews no option but to exact usury (*würdt inen der ungötlich zynss abgon, den sie jährlich aus inen schäzen, und sie also zum wucher ursachend . . .*).[18]

It was precisely this point which Luther's 1523 writing on the Jews drove home, this time against the spiritual authorities. His criticism of past policies toward the Jews is one link in a chain of evidence documenting ecclesiastical oppression and misguidedness; but it is not, however, as it is so often wrongly construed, a call for Jewish emancipation. Erasmus struck the same note in the phrase quoted earlier which, on the surface, looks so emancipatory on the surface: "If hating the Jews is the proof of a truly Christian life, then we are all excellent Christians."[19] This moral reproach, which clearly has its direct parallel in the Luther of 1523,[20] coexists without contradiction or strain beside Erasmus's lifelong, deeply rooted anti-Jewish convictions.[21] But since it is uphill work connecting the Dutchman with the history of the Third Reich, he has never been embroiled in the apologetic attempt to remodel the Luther of 1523 as a Jewish sympathizer. Here, too, the isolation of the great Wittenberg reformer has brought forth evil fruit, for Erasmus could have set things straight: Judaism has not been upgraded; Christianity is under attack. This offensive was, to be sure, something new in the spirit of the times—and Erasmus and Luther were perfectly aware of that.

10

Regensburg 1519:
Urban Expulsion and Social Protest

One revealing component of sixteenth-century anti-Jewish agitation is the brief saga of the history of Jewish expulsions, which was routinely adduced by way of justification above all in the pamphlets on urban expulsions. The listing of deportations was intended to serve as evidence of a pan-European Christian consensus; the objective was to teach the authorities of any region that was "still" inhabited by Jews, or of a city that was "unfortunately not yet" Jew-free, how at long last to implement measures that were "necessary" and "way overdue."

During the early Reformation, the question of Jewish toleration was still an open one in a few territories like Saxony or Hessen. In the major urban areas, however, expulsion was by that time nearly complete. As one of the last of a long line of cities, Regensburg decided on 21 February 1519—during Lent, as usual an explosively dangerous time for Jews—to put an abrupt end (within four days) to its Jewish ghetto, one of the largest and oldest in the empire. Not only in the pamphlets of the 1520s was the drama of Regensburg eagerly paraded as a "crowning achievement," but even modern scholarship has by preference concentrated on Regensburg, only partially because of the city's excellent source materials and the preeminent collection of documents assembled by Raphael Strauss.[22]

One can hardly escape anachronistic "remote control" inferences: the striking parallels between Regensburg and Ravensbrück. But the histories of the post–Third Reich period are not alone congenitally prone to distortion. The parallels were laid out in programmatic form decidedly earlier by Wilhelm Grau in his 1934 monograph on Regensburg, *Antisemitismus im späten Mittelalter*[23] (*Antisemitism in the Late Middle Ages*). The first sentence of the foreword at once conveys the aspirations of National Socialist days: "More so than any other discipline, history is bound to collaborate in the political education of our nation."[24] To lend credence to this preamble, Grau invokes the plea of Johan Huizinga, the great liberal historian: "The Jewish question has been a problem in every hour of Western and principally of German history, unmitigated and unresolved. . . . When will it be possible to solve it once and for all?"[25] The "final solution" here proclaims itself—for the first time in the German language, no doubt—with a stately academic air.

Over and against the racist interpretation, religous and economic factors have been favored since World War II.[26] But both the Nazi slant and the supposedly nonideological refutation of the race thesis demand and absorb so much scholarly energy that access to the age of the sixteenth century, which the pamphlets might well broaden, has actually been blocked. Ironically, the abstract debate by historians over such exalted problems as "historically transcendent causalities" has provoked, by way of reprisal, research into the more intimate conditions of life, the more concrete aspects, and attention to the "common man" through intensive study of the pamphlet literature, reports, and brief chronicles.

The incidents of Regensburg find their real significance in such "intimate" sources. It becomes apparent here that the events should not be limited to a local history or confined to a separate, specialized history of the Jews in Germany. With source material of this caliber, we are in a position to approach the Jewish question of the sixteenth century from something more than the perspective of individual, exceptional figures, even if our hope of an audience with "the man on the street" is vain.

At the "intermediate level," between the wholly rarified and entirely commonplace, two things become clear. First, expulsion is very closely tied to the social unrest of both city and countryside up to the Peasants' War (1524–26). Second, the new tendencies and evaluations discernible in the intellectual vanguard now recede into the background. Instead, at this same intermediate level, with its polemics and agitation, we discover how the late Middle Ages, striding with unbroken continuity over the threshold of the new era, persists in all its vitality directly into the sixteenth century. So we must dismiss the stubborn thesis of discontinuity which, based on Regensburg, pervades the scholarship devoted to the Jewish expulsions and which, since Grau, has remained unchallenged: "On the threshold of the Reformation, which spurned the cult of the Virgin, and under the guidance of men who a few years later became passionate advocates of the new dogma, there now emerged in Regensburg a full-blown cult of the Virgin; suffused with the colors of medieval spirituality, it was deliberately displayed as a symbol of triumph over the Jews and interwoven with material interests and political designs. The medieval world, at the end of its strength, again lifted its head to spend itself utterly this one last time, and then to sink back in exhaustion."[27]

The medieval world proved to be anything but exhausted, let alone "at the end of its strength." The contemporary preacher of Regensburg, Balthasar Hubmaier (d. 1528),[28] succeeded in mobilizing the masses against the patrician pro-imperial faction in the city council. To this end, he could count on the readily intelligible, tried and "true" anti-Jewish arguments of his day: social protest, current in all parts of Europe, here fuses with anti-Jewish sentiment to yield a highly volatile and potent form of political agitation. The city chronicler Christoph Hoffmann offers a vivid record of this polemic in his description (10 June 1519) of the events that scarcely five months earlier led to the Lenten expulsion of the Jews from Regensburg. In the face of early resistance and imperial prohibition, the great Doctor Hubmaier, undaunted, proclaims the Word of God against that race which is at once "idle, lecherous, and greedy."[29] Like a good shepherd, Hubmaier places himself before the sheep of Christ. As God in his mercy had led him toward Regensburg as a prophet,[30] so too the prophet in his mercy exposes the Jews as a plague upon the city, bravely exhorting their expulsion from Regensburg.[31]

The impact of this fiery street sermon can be gauged from the reaction of Hubmaier's flock upon learning of the council's expulsion decree. The population, streaming together, gave thanks with tears of joy—thus Hoffman—that Jesus Christ had kept watch over his suffering people and freed wretched Regensburg from the perfidious Jews. Expulsion becomes literally emancipation: *Liberare et emancipare*! As for the Jews, they are idle, lecherous, and greedy: *otio, venerique usurisque deditum*.[32] This latter charge was soon leveled with increasing harshness against the mendicant friars and thereafter against orthodoxy in general.

Though the language is Latin and the genre that of the concise, factual chronical,[33] the tone of Hoffman's firsthand report, in its concluding segment absorbs the frenzy of upheaval which then raged at the threshold of the Reformation. Hubmaier's resounding impact was not the product of rhetorical force, as Hoffman insists. His effectiveness stemmed from the persistence of medieval eschatology accompanied by the hope that God would directly intervene and would, at the end of days, call forth a new prophet whose preaching would vanquish once and for all the reign of the godless.

Alongside this apocalyptic anticipation of a new Elijah,[34] Hoffman could without difficulty propagate another unmistakably medieval tradition. This was the massive polemic against the Jews, spearheaded above all by the mendicant friars with arguments that would soon recoil upon the monks themselves. A precursor and model for Hoffman's chronicle can be found most notably in the crude anti-Jewish marketplace sermon of the Dominican Peter Schwarz (Niger), dating from the year 1474, and published the following year in Esslingen and Nuremberg.[35] Even sharper than Schwarz's tirade was the "Description of the Atrocities of the Jews," the *Fortalitium fidei* of the Franciscan Alfonsus de Spina (d. 1469) composed in 1460 and printed for the first time in Strasbourg in 1471, with a series of reprintings in Basel, Nuremberg, and Lyon (1511).[36] The refrain of the these anti-Jewish writings was invariably the same: the murderers of God are not only opponents of the church, they are the plague of society; unsatisfied simply with the death of Christ, they covet Christian wealth and blood.

A third medieval bestseller, likewise available in Regensburg at the time, carried, it should be stressed, directly over into the age of Reformation—the widely circulated *Epistola de adventu Messiae*,[37] translated into German in 1523 by Ludwig Hätzer under the title *Ain beweysung das der war Messias kommen sei*[38] (*A Demonstration That the True Messiah Is Come*). An intellectual ally of Hubmaier and like him a pupil of Zwingli, Hätzer had already broken with the latter by 1524 when his tract appeared, shot through with insults. It was not the Jews who from now on would draw the fire of Hätzer's reforming critique, but the city council of Zurich, which had declined to prohibit the charging of interest. When the council balked, Hätzer went his own Anabaptist way;[39] and in the second edition of the *Beweysung*, Zwingli fell under the cross wires. The great victim of the intra-Christian intolerance of the sixteenth century, the so-called left wing of the Reformation, originally the Anabaptists, were anything but Jewish sympathizers; they were a part of that intermediate stratum of the small, non-self-supporting handworkers who, as much as a century earlier, had begun to encourage the municipal harassment of Jews.

Just how closely fused were social protest and anti-Jewish sermonizing becomes evident once again in the proceedings of the council of Regensburg in 1518 in the matter of the Franciscan, Conrad Schwarz. It appears that Schwarz's sermon against usury, interest, and market manipulation had in fact been addressed not only against Jews, but against the city council as well. Conrad Schwarz was arraigned for having incited rebellion on the long-since dubious grounds: those things which are needed by all belong to all (*in necessitate omnia sunt communia*). On 16 May 1525, this maxim would form the nucleus of Thomas Müntzer's forced confession under torture.[40]

11

Agitation and Jew-Baiting

The observations made up to now about the uses of agitation and propaganda can be condensed into the following four points.

1. Pamphlets in general are a pre-Reformation medium that cannot be viewed apart from the so-called Reformation pamphlets, with regard to form or content. In their potential for agitation, pamphlets should obviously not be considered a discovery of the sixteenth century. The anti-Jewish pamphlets in particular are of late medieval origin.

2. With regard to the spread of the Reformation, the following statement holds without qualification: "*Viva voce* proclamation of the gospel was immeasurably assisted by the flood of pamphlets."[41] Without a doubt, printing production stepped up rapidly in the sixteenth century, although the coupling of (itinerant) sermons and pamphlets was atypical of the early modern age. But it *was* typical of the late Middle Ages. Beyond this, it must be kept in mind that the genre of the sermon both antedates and accompanies the pamphlets. Multiplying by word of mouth, the sermon in turn reached the illiterate segments by means of personal address with more penetrating effect than the pamphlets could muster. The efficient union of sermon and pamphlet not only gave impetus to the Reformation but also, in times not so far back, accelerated the expulsion of the Jews.

3. The emotional core at which the agitational literature aims is not exclusively the *Angst* so much in vogue today. The dread, and therefore the hope inseparably bound up with it, was actually focused on the approaching doomsday, the menace of the devil's power and the judgment of God. To the extent, however, that "data" expose causes—to the extent that disasters can be traced to and explained by human failures—the pamphlets sought to convert fear into rage by aiming inflammatory "information" against Jews, the

government, or the church. This rage in turn became a source of energy for storming the barricades along the way to a reform of church and society.

4. Modern interest in the pamphlets is sustained by our hopes of grasping in them the very roots of an unstructured, primal, and spontaneous popular sentiment removed from all sophisticated abstraction and direction "from above." Whether we really can make this approximation remains questionable. As with the numerous, still extant sermons, so too with the pamphlets: we know only what was brought to the market, not what was actually bought.

Moreover, in the insurgent efforts to capitalize upon issues aired in the streets and in the pubs, goal-orientation and instruction "from above" are indeed to be taken seriously.[42] Without information, no agitation. In other words, even pamphlets are instruments of control. The "spontaneous" popular rage we hear about again and again is not simply a matter of popular religion or a "grassroots" groundswell, as is evident in the *Judenspiegel*. Quite the contrary: the pamphlets mark a consciously engineered continuation of the medieval penitential sermon, though now with a new orientation. The focus is not the sins of the individual but the "crimes" of society. The rhetoric is all the more vehement because the battle no longer concerns the enemy without, but the enemy harbored within—first the Jews, then the monks and priests, and finally the "bigwigs" taken as a whole.

12

Fear of the Jews:
Between Piety and Superstition

In our earlier test cases—Pfefferkorn, Luther, and Regensburg—the structural and substantive parallels between Jew-hatred, anticlericalism, and criticism of authority became clear. Complaints and grievances against clerics and especially against mendicant friars were first rehearsed in the confrontation with the "idle, lecherous, and greedy" Jews. This occurs already in Pfefferkorn, with his surprisingly explicit criticism of authorities who protect Jews.

This observation has implications for any modern historical account that adopts a partisan perspective. In measuring the pamphlets and other writings on the Jews against a modern scale of values, the postwar historian has generally taken the side of the oppressed and virtually disenfranchised Jews. With regard to social questions, the same "liberal" historian is thoroughly inclined to condemn the governing bodies as conservative and autocratic while, on the other hand, portraying the opposition represented by the guilds or the restless masses as progressive, trend-setting, and proto-democratic. But when he is now confronted with the phenomenon of an authority that is protective of Jews, his scale of values looks very much the product of a modern perspective that tends to oversimplify, and even overmoralize, the historical circumstances.

There is another facet to this modern perspective: regardless of whether the sixteenth century is filed under "the early modern era" or the "age of Humanism and Reformation," there always lurks the background suggestion that the Middle Ages is over with, or at the very least on its last legs. A corollary of this assumption is the previously cited thesis that the Jewish expulsion in Regensburg was accompanied by a last, sudden blossoming of the cult of the Virgin, which was then quickly eclipsed. Our intention is not to cast judgment on true and false piety, but rather to establish the fact that piety—and, if correctly understood, the veneration of the Mother of God as well—is not something specifically medieval that is then, finally, "overcome." On the contrary, piety stamps and conditions the early modern era with as much force as do political and social interests.

The Mother of God and the ever-virgin Mary consistently played a most prominent role throughout the dialogues with Jews. There existed hardly a debate in which a Jew did not point out that the translation from Isa. 7:14—"Behold, a virgin shall conceive and bear a son, and shall call his name Immanuel"—was erroneous, since the Hebrew word *'alma* meant not "virgin" but (as is generally recognized today) "young woman." This objection, launched against a text crucial to Christian claims on Old Testament prophecy, unleashed from the Christian side a proliferation of curses, since Mary, untouched and unsullied (*intacta et immaculata*),[43] had been prefigured ages ago in the bush that burned and was not consumed (Exodus 3). Just as the bush was not reduced to ashes but remained unscathed as God, in its flames, manifested himself to Moses, so too did Mary remain exempt from all sin when God entered the world. And since the miraculous appearance of God—against all the laws of nature—must be quite familiar to the Jews from their own Old Testament, their ignorance was considered not blindness, but a wicked and diabolical denial that had to be combated.[44] In the anti-Jewish sermons intended for popular ears and widely disseminated in pamphlet form, disparagement of the Mother of God often weighed heavier than thefts of the host, ritual murders, and—still only occasionally—well poisoning.

The customary portrait of medieval Mariology concludes with a dispute between the proponents of Mary's own immaculate conception and their opponents in the Dominican orders who maintained that the mother of the Lord was conceived in a state of human sin. Specialized literature will mention if need be the public climax of the dispute, the Jetzer scandal in Bern, when in 1509 four Dominicans were condemned to death by fire for criminal blasphemy. Three years previously they had induced a journeyman tailor named Jetzer to spread the story that the Mother of God had personally appeared to him and attested to her sinful, human conception.[45] Where the beginnings of the Reformation are of primary concern, these scandals and disputes today appear antiquated, while Mariology has relevance at best in the history of theology—a residuum from a previous era, surviving only in the privacy of personal devotion and habit. This view is untenable and misleading, for the Marian devotion obviously articulates social tensions.[46] In specifically Franciscan popular sermons, by analogy to St. Francis's "marriage" with the virgin lady "Poverty," the spotless, humble handmaiden Mary becomes a universal symbol for the outcasts, the poor, and the needy. In the hymn of praise to Mary, the *Magnificat*, the passage from Luke 1:52—"He hath put down the mighty from their thrones"— acquired an explosive power that could at any moment be detonated in the name of radical reform, Reformation, or even revolution. This disruptive force serves the Reformation in various ways.[47] We see it in Luther already in 1519,[48] and in Müntzer increasingly until his death in 1525.[49]

Balthasar Hubmaier, too, carried his point against the Regensburg Council in February of 1519; he reasserted the Jewish defamation of Mary so insistently that in the shortest imaginable time the synagogue was destroyed and in its place a chapel to Mary erected by the joint efforts of a population held in the grip of a true Mary-psychosis. Similar events occurred entirely independently of Hubmaier in Bamberg, Nuremberg, Rothenburg, and Würzburg.[50] Clearly, we have detected the spirit of the times.

Although the bridge from piety to superstition has at last been brought into clearer view, the gray zone of fear and persecution remains impenetrable. The accusations of desecration of the sacraments and ritual murder in fact prepared the ground for the eruption of full-scale witch hunts that followed the Jewish expulsions. While the *Witches' Hammer (Malleus Maleficarum*, written around 1487),[51] the official witch-hunter's manual, has received thorough investigation in recent years, a parallel text has until now been overlooked: the *Pharetra catholicei fidei*, literally the "quiver," but more to the point, the "hammer of Jews" of the Catholic faith. With a circulation far exceeding that of the *Witches' Hammer* in sheer geographic terms, the *Pharetra*, published eight years later, also enjoyed a greater number of printings, very likely because its intended readership was not confined alone to learned theologians and authorized Inquisitors. Hans Folz (1513) of Nuremberg, the master singer and printer of his own works designed especially for the skilled handcrafters' guilds, composed a still-more-ferocious German version.[52] The unpretentious Latin of the work, however, permitted its use in the original by ordinary clerics whose linguistic skills were limited to their liturgical Latin.

While the *Malleus* was written by two Dominicans, the *Pharetra* betrays glaring Franciscan influences, above all in the sensitive area of Mariology. The brief work poses, in the form of a disputation, the kinds of questions and answers conducive not to converting Jews, but to convicting them, and better yet, with their own weapons, the Old Testament: "This is how we can best confute the worthless Jews who have been repulsed by God and therefore are utterly abject. . . ."⁵³ The unbiased, objective diction of the Jewish interlocutor stands in sharp contrast to the heated, aggressive, and insulting retorts of the Christian opponent. The debate closes with a prayer by the Jew that sounds utterly ambiguous, even ironic, and not to modern ears only: "May God convert us all (*nos omnes*) and lead us onto the path of righteousness. . . ."⁵⁴ The Christian champion cuts such a supercilious, injurious, and even libelous figure that the reader feels he is participating rather in a denunciation than in a search for truth, a mock trial instead of a dialogue.

This contrast is particularly pronounced in light of the decorous intercessor for Judaism who, with scholarly precision, courteous in manner and impartial in substance, broaches the very problems of the Trinity, the incarnation of Christ, and the Eucharist, whose scriptural foundation has been debated through the whole history of theology. This same Jew is labeled "obdurate, public menace, dumb mule"; he is the spirit that perpetually denies, soulless, soul's bane, in sum, the factotum of the devil.

Clearly the *Pharetra* is far from being a pastoral primer. It is a manual for condemning Jews. In fact, it is not greatly interested in the Jews, but rather in a Christianity that is menaced by the devil. At stake is not victory, but exorcism. The Jew tramples upon God's kingdom, since he denies God's presence in Christ, in the church, and in the sacrament, and hence repudiates God's sovereignty. As is usual in the genre of writings "against the perfidious Jews" (*contra perfidos Judaeos*),⁵⁵ which derives from the medieval "Jewish sermon," so too in the *Pharetra* are blasphemy against the Virgin, profanation of the host, and ritual murder presumed to be "typically Jewish" as well as actual occurrences whose factualness is supported by "historical" documentation.

Given the aforementioned disparities, it is understandable that the *Malleus* and the *Pharetra* have never before been juxtaposed for comparison. But once we perceive the parallels between the two and recognize that the *Witches' Hammer* and the *Jews' Hammer*⁵⁶ are manuals for demolition, then it becomes obvious that in this respect, too, the anti-Jewish polemic and the expulsion of Jews do not represent a last recrudescence of an already weary medieval piety. They herald not an ending, but a horror-laden beginning.

Notes to Part Two

1. The prehistory of anti-Semitism is not restricted to the early Christian or medieval periods. Augustine (*De civitate Dei*, VI. 1, CCSL 47, 183, 10) cites without hesitation Seneca's unambivalent designation of the Jews as an exceedingly criminal race—*sceleratissima gens* (*De superstitione*, ca. A.D. 65). For Seneca's place in classical letters see *Greek and Latin Authors on Jews and Judaism*, ed. M. Stern (Jerusalem, 1974), 1: 429f.

2. In a revealing and substantial analysis of the so-called *historie avant-garde*, the social historian Lawrence Stone replies to the prophecy made by Le Roy Ladurie in 1968: "In 1980 every historian will have to have become a programmer, if he is to survive," with the observation: "This was a failed prophecy if ever there was one. . . . Most historians count today, but only when it seems appropriate, and whenever possible we try to keep away from the computer as a dangerously time-consuming tool with strictly limited potentialities for the manipulation of such imprecise data as historical evidence" (L. Stone, "In the Alleys of Mentalité," *The New York Review of Books* 26 [1979]: 20–24; 21).

3. See the rich and useful volume *Flugschriften als Massenmedium der Reformationszeit. Beiträge zum Tübinger Symposium 1980*, ed. v. H.-J. Köhler (Stuttgart, 1981). For the first version of Part Two, with extensive documentation, see my contribution to this collection, 269–89.

4. See my introduction to *Werden und Wertung der Reformation. Vom Wegestreit zum Glaubenskampf, Spätscholastik und Reformation 2*, 2d ed. (Tübingen, 1979), x.

5. A collection of the Pfefferkorn writings can be found in Eduard Böcking, *Hutteni Opera, Supp. Bd. 2* (Leipzig, 1869), 53–115.

6. See above, 24–25.

7. See Johannes Pfefferkorn, *Judenspiegel* (Cologne, 1507), fol. C 4^v–D 1^r.

8. *Augenspiegel* (Tübingen, 1511), fol. A 5^r; reprinted in *Quellen zur Geschichte des Humanismus und der Reformation in Faksimile-Ausgaben*, vol. 5 (München, [1961]).

9. A continuously updated bibliography can be found in the *Luther-jahrbuch* under the section heading "5h."

10. WA 11: 315, 3.

11. Cf. Scott H. Hendrix, *Ecclesia in via. Ecclesiological Developments*

in the Medieval Psalms Exegesis and the Dictate super psalterium (1513–1515) of Martin Luther (Leiden, 1974), 249–56.

12. "... here comes a new fruit, a Lutheristic one, that wants to doctor up the child murders of the Jews" (Johannes Eck, *Ains Judenbüechlins Verlegung* [Ingolstadt, 1542; first ed., 1541], fol. N 4^r).

13. Johannes Eberlin von Günzburg, *Sämtliche Schriften*, ed. L. Enders, 3 vols. *Flugschriften aus der Reformationszeit* 11, 15, 18 (Halle, 1896–1902), 3: 111–24; cf. XXIV–XXVI, 346–48. See also Karl Steiff, *Der erste Buchdruck in Tübingen (1498–1534). Ein Beitrag zur Geschichte der Universität* (Tübingen, 1881; reprint ed., Nieuwkoop, 1953), Nachträge 18, no. 4 (Eberlin, 111):

> Der Clocker thurn bin ich genant
> Vñ meld hie d'võ güntzburg schand
>   Wie wohl ich nur ein Steinhauff bin
> Zwingt mich doch des euãgelistẽ sin
>   Dañ sie mich habend missgebraucht
>   Mit mir gestrafft den armen hauff
> Dem christus selb sein wort verheisst
>   Als Lucas klar am siebenden weisst
> Wo fischer schnitzer bierwirt regiert
>   Die pollici wirdt leicht zerstört.

14. Günzburg, *Samtliche Schriften,* 3: 124, cf. 348.

15. Ibid., 120.

16. Ibid., 117.

17. Ibid., 113f.; cf. 347n. In the summons of the second Diet at Nuremberg it was resolved that "in time nothing other than the Holy Gospel, the interpretation of the Scriptures by the Christian Church, shall be approved and acceptable for sermonizing" (*Deutsche Reichstagsakten unter Kaiser Karl V.,* ed. A. Wrede [Gotha, 1901], 3: 746f.). Cf. *Werden und Wertung* (see n. 4 above), 249 n. 28=*Masters of the Reformation,* 196 n. 28.

18. Günzburg, *Samtliche Schriften,* 3:114; cf. 347. Cf. the progressive legislation on Jews in the Wolfaria pamphlet *(Der 11. Bundsgenoss); ibid.,* 1: 130f.

19. *Opus Epistolarum Des. Erasmi Roterodami,* ed. P. S. Allen et al., 12 vols. (New York: Oxford University Press, 1906–47 [= Allen]), 4: 46, 142f. Letter to Hochstraten, 11 August 1519.

20. "Si odium Iudaeorum et haereticorum et Turcorum facit Christianos, vere nos etiam furiosi sumus omnium christianissimi. Si autem amor Christi facit Christianos, sine dubio nos peiores Iudaeis, haereticis et Turcis sumus, cum nemo Christum amet minus quam nos"(*WA* 5: 429, 9–13[Ps. 14:7; 1519]). The expansion of the list here to include heretics and Turks (not present in Erasmus) should be noted.

21. See Guido Kisch, *Erasmus' Stellung zu Juden und Judentum* (Tübingen, 1969), 29. In a noteworthy essay, Cornelis Augustijn has tried to cripple the arguments of Kisch: "Erasmus und die Juden," *Nederlands Archief voor Kerkgeschiedenis* 60 (1980): 22–38. Simon Markish's *Erasme et les Juifs* (Lausanne, 1979) offers no new insights on the discussion. It is undeniable that Erasmus is "anti-Judaistic" insofar as he wages a battle of the *spiritus contra literam*—but he is also capable of rejoicing in the fact that France is "Jew-free." See 38 above.

22. *Urkunden und Aktenstücke zur Geschichte der Juden in Regensburg 1453–1738,* ed. R. Strauss (München, 1960).

23. Wilhelm Grau, *Antisemitismus im späten Mittelalter* (München, 1934; 2d ed., 1939).

24. Karl Alexander von Müller, "Zum Geleit," in ibid., V.

25. Ibid., VII. Only the following sentence, originally intended so differently, remains true: "German historiography lacks many times over the courage to unfold the full historical problematics of the Jewish question" (ibid., 193 n. 8, with a commentary on the previous literature). Cf. the spiteful remarks on 194f. nn. 24, 39.

26. "The sermons against usury and the right to contraband were of lasting and decisive importance in the formation of anti-Jewish sentiment" (Peter Herde, "Gestaltung und Krisis des christlich-jüdischen Verhältnisses in Regensburg am Ende des Mittelalters," in *Zeitschrift für Bayerische Landesgeschichte* 22 [1959]: 359–95; 384).

27. Grau, *Antisemitismus im späten Mittelalter,* 160.

28. Cf. Torsten Bergsten, *Balthasar Hubmaier. Seine Stellung zu Reformation und Täufertum 1521–1528* (Kassel, 1961), 76–86; Christof Windhorst, *Täuferisches Taufverständnis. Balthasar Hubmaiers Lehre zwischen traditioneller und reformatorischer Theologie* (Leiden, 1976), 7, 25.

29. *De Ratisbona metropoli boioariae et subita ibidem iudaeorum proscriptione* (Regensburg, 1519), fol. C II^v.

30. Cf. the abridged version in R. Straus, *Urkunden,* 385, no. 1040.

31. "... ut bonus pastor murum se pro ovibus posuit, tactus dolore cordis intrinsecus, audenter contra hos nauci homines (ad nil aliud utiles quam ut in clibanum mittantur) praedicando, declamando fraudemque eorum sine intermissione detegendo . . ." (*De Ratisbone,* fol. C III^r).

32. Ibid., fol. C IV^v; C II^v.

33. It is chiefly a *laudatio* [!] of Regensburg: "inter totius nostrae Germaniae urbes laudatissima" (ibid., fol. A III^r). The chronicle is dedicated to an Augustinian monk.

34. See Christoph Peter Burger, "Endzeiterwartung im späten Mittelalter," in *Der Antichrist und Die Fünfzehn Zeichen vor dem Jüngsten Gericht* (Hamburg, 1979), 18–78; 35–38.

35. *Contra perfidos Iudaeos de conditionibus veri Messiae,* Hain, vol. 2.1, 506, no. 11885.

36. *Fortalitium fidei contra fidei Christianae hostes Alphonsi a Spina 1459.* Eduard Böcking, who furnishes additional information, relativizes the correct but harsh characterization of H. Graetz with the introductory words: "The Jew (!) H. Graetz does not exactly applaud Spina and his Fortalicium" (E. Böcking, *Ulrichi Hutteni Opera,* Suppl. vol. II [Leipzig, 1869], 372).

37. *Epistola ad Rabbi Isaac de Adventu Messiae, quem Iudaei temere expectant, Panzer,* vol. II, no. 2454. Presumedly written around 1072 by Rabbi Samuel Marrochiamus in Arabic as a declaration of the bankruptcy of the Jewish faith, and first translated and published in 1339, in a short time the *Epistola* attained great popularity, and was adopted and fitted admirably well into the program for Jewish missions.

38. Augsburg, January 1524; Zürich, March 1524.

39. Cf. J. F. Gerhard Goeter's *Ludwig Hätzer (ca. 1500 bis 1529). Spiritualist und Antitrinitarier. Eine Randfigur der frühen Täuferbewegung*

(Gütersloh, 1957), 36ff.: the second edition already alludes to the rift.

40. P. Herde, "Gestaltung und Krisis" (see n. 26 above), app. II, 394f. Cf. Thomas Müntzer, *Schriften und Briefe*, ed. G. Franz (Gütersloh, 1968), 548, 15.

41. Walter Peter Fuchs in Bruno Gebhardt, *Handbuch der deutschen Geschichte*, 9th ed. (Stuttgart, 1970), 2: 57.

42. Two pamphlets come to mind, both of which are clearly aimed at disseminating the ideas contained in Luther's *Jesus Christ Was Born a Jew* (1523). The first, Michael Kramer's *Eyn underredung von glawben* (Erfurt [2 December], 1523), in *Flugschriften aus den ersten Jahren der Reformation*, ed. O. Clemen (Halle, 1906/7; reprint ed., 1967), 1: 425–40, is rather simplistic. More skillful, and original, is *Ein gesprech auf das kurtzt zwuschen eynem Christen und Juden* (Erfurt, 1524), in ibid., 389–420.

43. See the "Pharetra catholice fidei siue ydonea disputatio inter Christianos et Judeos: in qua perpulchra tanguntur media et rationes, quibus quivis christifidelis tam ex prophetis suis propriis quam ex nostris eorum erroribus faciliter poterit obviare" ([1495], Landshut, 1514; fol. A III^{r-v}). Cf. n. 52 below.

44. "Disgrace and effrontery done by the Jews to the image of Mary, which had been commissioned by Maximilian the Holy Roman Emperor as a lasting monument, in the praiseworthy city of Cologne, from which they have also been eternally banished" ([Strasbourg: Matthias Hupfuff (?) around 1515], university library, Tübingen; call no.: Gh 415. 8°). Adam Klassert and Meier Spanier date this pamphlet to the year 1515 and attribute it with good reason to Thomas Murner. Cf. A. Klassert, "Entehrung Mariä durch die Juden. Eine antisemitische Dichtung Thomas Murners," *Jahrbuch für Geschichte, Sprache und Literatur Elsass-Lothringens* 21 (1905): 78–155; idem, "Zu Thomas Murners Entehrung Mariä durch die Juden," *Jahrbuch für Geschichte, Sprache und Literatur Elsass-Lothringens* 22 (1906): 255–75; M. Spanier, "Thomas Murners Beziehungen zum Judentum," *Elsass-Lothringisches Jahrbuch* 11 (1932); 89–108. The Franciscan Thomas Murner (d. 1537) was judged to be a partisan of Reuchlin by Johannes Pfefferkorn (cf. *Beschirmung Johannes Pfefferkorn*, [1516], fol. L III^{v}). Pfefferkorn's patrons, the Dominicans of Cologne, must have viewed Murner as an opponent because of his unsparing treatment of the Jetzer scandal in Bern, in his satire, *Von den fier ketzeren* (Strasbourg[?], 1509). Actually Murner may well have been friendly with one of the authors of the *Letters of Obscure Men*, presumably Hutten. In his attitude to the Jews he is not far from the position of the anti-Jewish agitation prevalent among the mendicant friars, as his glorification of the expulsion of Jews from Colmar in his tract, "Disgrace and effrontery, . . ." indicates. The intent of the entire pamphlet is to depict anti-Jewish sentiment and, even more, the expulsion and annihilation of Jews, as Christian obligations that receive their justification through proofs that Jews have perpetrated blasphemous atrocities.

45. Cf. Hans von Greyerz, "Der Jetzerprozess und die Humanisten," *Archiv des Historischen Vereins des Kantons Bern* 31 (1932): 243–99.

46. In the case of Johannes Teuschlein, Luke 1:52 (see the following note) plays a lesser role than does the idea, widely accepted since Bernard of Clairvaux, that Mary, as the *colla,* the connecting member between the head and the rest of the body, is the channel through which mercy flows: "Along

Flavius Mithridates. For Lollio's familiarity with Mithridates see the critical edition: Flavius Mithridate *Sermo de Passione Domini,* ed. C. Wirszubski (Jerusalem: Israel Academy of Humanities and Sciences, 1963), app. VII, 75f. See also Part One, n. 25 above.

56. The *Malleus* explicitly justifies the connection between witches and Jews with reference to the fact that both are guilty of apostasy (*Malleus* [cf. n. 51], Iq 14, 131). Witches and Jews alike should be punished by the secular arm with the confiscation of property and with capital punishment, since they resist the Christian faith (ibid., III, praefatio, 350, with an appeal to the Canon *De Iudeis* in *Decretum Gratiani* [c. 5 D. XLV, Friedberg, 1: 162]). In contrast to the *Malleus,* however, the *Decretum* rules out the use of violence against *unbaptized* Jews.

"Experience" too confirms the connection between Jews and witches. The assistance of a Jew was called upon to transform an unwilling, chaste virgin into a mare (*Malleus* Iq 10, 108). A baptized Jewess with her arts seduced other women into blaspheming the Virgin Mary and the birth of Christ (ibid., II cap. 12, 250f.). Among the innumerable implicit parallels, the following stand out: the search of witches for blood (Iq 16, 141); the theft of the consecrated Host (II cap. 5, 208); and child-sacrifice (II cap. 13, 254). The Ritual Phrase "the all-holy Virgin Mary is a fat wench" is the prerequisite for the initiation of a witch through a pact with the Devil (II cap. 2, 176; cf. also *Werden und Wertung,* as in n. 4 above, 201–33=*Masters of the Reformation,* 158–83).

In 1535 Philipp of Allendorf published the following: *The Jews' bathhouse: a demonstration of their trade's many dangers, as a warning to Christians, that they shun and avoid these deceptive snares.* Although primarily aimed in the present context at checking the "blood-letting" practiced by Jews in their usury, the "antibath syndrome" (against heretics, witches, and prostitutes) draws upon older associations as well. The *Malleus* expressly warns against these Bademütter (bathwenches): II cap. 1, 171f.; esp. cap. 15, 268f.

MARTIN LUTHER

The Jews as
Benefactors and Malefactors

If the apostles, who were also Jews, had dealt
with us Gentiles as we Gentiles have dealt with the
Jews, no Christians would ever have emerged
from among the Gentiles.

> Martin Luther,
> *Jesus Christ Was Born A Jew*
> (1523; *Weimarer Ausgabe* 11:315. 19–21)

Now what ought we Christians to do with this
rejected and damned people, the Jews? . . . We have
to practice a fierce mercy in hopes that we can at least save
a few of them from the glowing flames. Vengeance
is out of the question. Revenge already hangs
on their necks, a thousand times worse than we could
wish on them.

> Martin Luther,
> *On the Jews and Their Lies*
> (1543; *Weimarer Ausgabe* 53:522. 29–30, 34–37)

13

Christian Anxiety
and the Jewish Scourge

The problem of "Germany and the Jews," a compulsive issue since
the events of the Third Reich, is elucidated if not resolved each day in
the cultural pages of the Western press by means of an increasingly
automatic reference to Luther's abiding influence.[1] This provocation
has proved more than a match particularly for that brand of Luther
veneration which was resolved to isolate the reformer from the
context of his age so as to exhibit him as the lonely prophet of
modernity. Luther's assessment of the Jewish question can only be
reached, however, by widening our focus from "Luther and the
Jews," a topic hopelessly bound up with private biography, to its
expanded historical equivalent, "the Jews in the age of Renaissance
and Reformation." It is also time that we faced the fact that the
Jewish question does not occupy a dark corner in Luther's work, but
a central place in his theology.

We find ourselves in the remarkable position, evidently, of having
to choose between two Luthers, the two Luther images that currently
are circulating before the public. The first of these is the bold reformer, the liberating theologian, the powerfully eloquent German—and this figure is "Jew-free." The other Luther is at best an
evil relation who preached hatred to the Germans, codified the truly
"German" sensibility, and wrote mainly about Jews—this Luther is
unquestionably an "anti-Semite." If we ever hope to encounter the
historical Luther, we will have to overcome this cleavage and
reinstate the Jewish question back in its original, contextual
framework of Luther's output and impact. This will involve more
than reworking the choice tidbits from Luther's writings on the Jews
already available in the steadily mounting flood of scholarly literature.

One preliminary warning: this proposed fresh look at Luther's thought on the Jews is not designed or even apt to "redeem" him after the fact. Judgment, however, should be reserved for the end of the process.

On the eve of the Reformation, the condition of the Jews in western Europe could have been accurately described in a single word, "misery," which the Old High German language had coined as the equivalent for "exile." Edward I effected the expulsion of the entire Jewish population from England. Although in France King Philip the Fair (1285–1314) decreed the expulsion simply of these "English" Jews, he went on to match this policy with so harsh a domestic equivalent that in 1516(?) Erasmus of Rotterdam could lavish upon France the highest of praise for its having outstripped all other countries in "neatly cleansing" the Jews from its kingdom. On 2 January 1494, King Ferdinand and Queen Isabella issued the expulsion mandate for all of Spain. Five years later, the Jews driven to Portugal had to flee once again, or else undergo baptism. But even these new Christians were subjected to pogroms that culminated in the dreadful massacre of Lisbon in 1506.[2]

Although the urban expulsions in the German Empire assumed frightening proportions in the fifteenth century, they were almost humane in comparison with the Jewish persecutions of the previous age, which flared up spontaneously "from below" and characteristically ended in plundering and murder. Thus, in Lent of 1349, the Jewish inhabitants of Thuringia, Gotha, Eisenach, Frankenhausen, and one month later, those of Erfurt were either killed or harassed to the point of self-immolation. In those days, during the great plague epidemic of Europe, justification was ordinarily found in "well-poisonings," but the real cause—an anonymous, "enlightened" chronicler of the fifteenth century adds—was more likely the deep financial debts of the entire population.[3]

By the eve of the Reformation, the wave of urban expulsions had reached an end. After 1520, Jews were sporadically expelled from a relatively small number of cities, compared with the earlier period from 1388 (Strasbourg) to 1519 (Regensburg, Rothenburg ob der Tauber), during which time nearly ninety expulsions had been carried out.[4] In the aspiring German territories, the Jewish policy wavered a while longer: In view of the growing power vacuum at the center of the empire, should the local prince stake his claim on the lucrative imperial protective rights in order to pocket for himself the high-yielding tax? Governing elites in the cities would favor this

THE ROOTS OF ANTI-SEMITISM

expedient. Or, to secure peace and tranquillity, should the Jews be expelled, as the guilds were demanding in the name of the Holy Mother Mary, with the object of combatting usury?

Since the days of Duke Eberhard the Bearded (d. 1496), Württemberg was officially "Jew-free," a legal status that was expressly confirmed as a privilege by Emperor Charles V at the Diet of Augsburg in 1530.[5] The Jews in this instance served as an occasion for Charles to reassert his traditional rights and document his imperial powers over and against the pressures for self-determination exerted by the princes. On 14 April 1519, the bishop of Speyer, George, duke of Bavaria (d. 1529), ordered a complete quarantine of the Jews in his diocese. As justification, he pointed out that they were after all "not humans, but dogs."[6] Hesse and Saxony did not toe the line laid down by the emperor, but instead steered an independent course in the 1530s: Philip, landgrave of Hesse, followed the counsel of the Strasbourg reformer Martin Bucer,[7] while the Saxon Elector John Frederick looked to Martin Luther for advice. Neither of these reformers was at pains to appeal to his sovereign's conscience and request an unlimited protectionism for Jews. Residence permits were issued only under strict conditions: work, discipline, and good behavior. In 1539, King Sigismund of Poland resorted to measures aimed not against newly converted Christians, as had been the case on the Iberian peninsula at the beginning of the century, but against the "new Jews."[8] A Jewish missionary offensive and a consequent debilitation of Christianity were feared.

This completes our outline sketch of the state of European expulsions in the sixteenth century and of the differentiated legal status of the imperial Jews, which was always poised in a precarious balance between the emperor and the princes, between the prince-bishops and the cities. It was in these unsteady, shifting circumstances that Luther's writings on Jews took effect. Even so, Germany was not made "Jew-free." The Jews who were expelled from the cities took refuge in the provinces where, apart from exceptional, isolated cases of displacement, they could take up residence without ever having to subject themselves to forced baptism. On the other hand, residence privileges, which were always provisional, and the never-predictable-because-decentralized policy of taxation translated into a constant pressure toward conversion. What ought to be striking is less the social and political discrimination than the strong sense of identity and capacity for survival demonstrated by the Jewish communities.

In addition to pressure from without, there was the pressure from within created by the defamation of the Jew as a morally degenerate and socially dangerous subject. The call for a thorough isolation of the Jewish community and the terrifying images that were publicly propagated against them were certain to promote a bitter hatred in the Jews toward Christians and their tyrannical faith—a hatred that smoldered the more deeply since the bitterness could have no outlet. Such a hatred was, on the other hand, so entirely probable to the Christians, whose credulity had been conditioned by their own sermons and by the "honest confessions" of baptized Jews, that horror stories about Jewish vindictiveness could find an instant audience. But reports of desecrations of the host and child murder circulated not only at the lowest level of the gutters and pubs, and not only in the sermons used by coarse-grained monks to whip up the passions of the mob.

The following document will demonstrate just how credible the hatred of alarmed Christians had made the counter-hatred of the Jews. We must keep in mind that this is hardly a piece of "sensational literature" from some shady provincial press, but rather a "serious" report styled after competent fact-finding commissions, convincingly effective in its precision of detail. The report was brought out by the publishing house of Hieronymous Höltzel of Nuremberg, a scholarly and politically progressive press in the service of Humanism and, later, of the Reformation.[9] Its repertoire included the works of the celebrated German authority on poetry, Conrad Celtis, a series of woodcuts by Albrecht Dürer, and later, works by Luther and Karlstadt, and even the harsh repudiation of Luther's Reformation by Thomas Müntzer in 1524, one year before the Peasants' War: the *Hochverursachte Schutzrede und Antwort wider das geistlose, sanftlebende Fleisch zu Wittenberg* ("A Most Justified Apology and Reply Against the Vacuous, Sybaritic Corpulence of Wittenberg"). Hieronymous Höltzel, both printer and publisher, was always one to stand on the front line.

An Incredible Event*

Jews from the Brandenburg Province purchase and torture the body of Christ in the year of our Lord 1510. Herewith is published what formerly has been common knowledge. The following occurred at 11:00 P.M. on the Wednesday after the Feast of the Purification of Mary.[10] Paul Fromm, a "wicked Christian"[11] and a native Pomeranian and resident of Bernau,[12] a tinker and a reputed murderer, let himself be tempted by the devil. In the church of Knoblauch,[13] Brandenburg, he broke into the tabernacle[14] at the altar, from which he stole a gilded pyx

---

* Due to the exemplary nature of the document, the original is given in the appendix.

containing two consecrated wafers, one large and one small, and one gilded monstrance[15] of copper. When, on the following day around eight o'clock in the morning, he sat down on a stone in the vicinity of Staaken[16] to inspect his plunder, he abused the larger wafer in an unworthy manner. Instantly he was plunged into pitch darkness, and he could neither get up nor move for over half an hour. Shortly afterwards, he headed to Spandau (two miles from Berlin, in the direction of Brandenburg, where the Havel and the Spree meet) and there offered to sell the monstrance to a Jew with the name Salomon. Salomon replied: "Where this is from, there are more." The wicked Christian then drew the sacrament from his breast pocket and demanded sixteen groschen. Salomon offered him five, and the deal was closed at nine district groschen, or six silver groschen.

Next, the man who had sold God headed toward the Wendische,[17] but as he did not wish to stay there, he returned home, heedless of the warning that his unconscionable theft was already notorious. Once home, he threw the monstrance from his house over the city wall, but with God's providence it hung in a tree. The burgomaster of Bernau found it there and had the already-suspect man taken into custody. The man confessed immediately, without torture.

Salomon had meanwhile laid the sacrament on the edge of a table and, out of congenital Jewish hatred, battered it several times over and pierced it; even then he was unable to wound the Lord's body. Finally, beside himself with rage, he yelled out, among other curses: "If you are the Christian God, then in the name of a thousand devils, show yourself!" At that moment, in reaction to the taunt, the holy body of Christ miraculously parted itself into three, just as the priest breaks it,—but with the result that the cracks took on the color of blood. The Jew carried the three parts of the wafer on his person for four weeks.

One year earlier, Salomon had agreed with the Brandenburg Jews, Jacob and Marcus (from Stendal),[18] that if one of them should manage to get hold of a sacramental wafer he would give each of the other two a share. And so Salomon now gave the two portions of the wafer, well packed in small boxes covered with Samian leather, to his son to take to Jacob in Brandenburg and to Marcus in Stendal.

The remaining piece, which was his own, he once again struck and pierced until blood flowed from it. He did everything he could to offend this last portion of the host—drowning it, burning it, and attempting in several other ways to destroy it—all to no avail. Finally it dawned on him to knead the sacrament into a scrap of matzo dough[19] and to throw it into the oven at the Jewish Easter celebration. And even though it was pitch black in this oven, all of a sudden he saw (as he himself confessed) a bright luminescence, and twice he saw floating above the bread a beautiful little child of a thumb's length. Deeply shocked at this miraculous event, and however much he wanted to fly from the spectre of the Christian prison before his eyes, it proved utterly impossible for him to move his legs and flee Spandau.

Marcus, the Jew from Stendal, likewise subjected the second portion of the wafer to all the tortures he could devise, and then sent it on to Braunschweig or, according to other reports, to Frankfurt am Main.

Similarly, Jacob of Brandenburg placed the third wafer portion on his table and gave it such a battering and piercing that one could see the grace-filled drops of blood on the table. As he could neither wash nor scratch away the blood, he knocked the blood-spattered chip from the table and took it and the wafer to Osterburg.[20] There an affluent Jew named Mayer gave the wafer to his son Isaac, who in turn brought the holy sacrament to his wife at the marriage bed with words to the effect that she should be truly thrilled and highly honored to know that he was bringing her the God of the Christians.

During the marriage feast, the enemies of Christ subjected the sacrament once again to torture. As bridegroom, Isaac had the honor of the first blow. This wafer is also said to have ended up in Braunschweig, where now all the Jews of that town are sitting in prison. The wafer and the blood-spattered chip together with the table were brought to Berlin. There the wafer miraculously turned into bread again, and then crumbled and slowly vanished.

While they were in jail, the obstinate, blind dogs confessed that in the past few years they had purchased seven Christian children, one from his own peasant mother for twenty-four groschen, another for three guilder, and a third for ten. These children they pierced with needles and knives, tortured, and finally killed them. Then they prepared the blood with pomegranates and served it for dinner.

On this account, his majesty, the noble Landgrave Joachim of Brandenburg,[21] sentenced the criminals to death on Friday after the fifteenth of July[22] in Berlin, and declared their personal belongings and holdings confiscate. The Christian, Paul Fromm, was to be shredded with tongs and burned on a separate stake. Next, thirty-eight Jews, chained by the neck, were to be burned to ashes.

And—one has to have seen it to believe it—these obstinate and impenitent Jews received their sentences with smug looks and were led away singing loud hosannas. Once on the stakes, they not only sang and laughed but some also danced and sent up shouts of jubilation, their chained hands raised high, crushing straw and stuffing it in their mouths. Without any regard for the manifest portents, they suffered their death unflinchingly, to the great horror of inconstant Christians.

Of the aforementioned Jews, Jacob and two others had themselves baptized. Jacob, whose Christian name is now Jörg, and one of the other two, were beheaded the next day and died Christians. The third, an occultist, was allowed at his own request to enter the Graue monastery in Berlin,[23] since his guilt was limited to crimes against children only.

Nearly sixty Jews live to this day in Berlin without any knowledge of these events. It is said they will be turned out of this territory again, as is only fitting and proper.

Printed at Nuremberg
by Hieronymous Höltzel

This document is its own commentary, both in the criminal details and in the vividness of the juxtaposed scenes.

We do not have at our disposal a Jewish version of the events; it would not, in any case, have been believed. The joyful display of courage and conviction by those Jews doomed to death could only arouse the ambivalent reaction of terror. When it comes to differentiating between truth and fiction, to extracting the actual kernel of these events, historical analysis founders. Even the admissions about the exact price tags of the sacraments and the children are not elicited from a wicked conscience. Paul Fromm, it is so tellingly said, confessed immediately, "without torture."

Christianity felt itself plagued and threatened: torture and execution of the Lord, torture and murder of children, public and—at the marriage bed—private blasphemies cried out for radical defense measures. For a Jew to live in exile was a perilous fate, even in those places like Berlin and Spandau where the "dear" privilege of residence was guaranteed—provisionally. Only thus did Jews realize that they were experiencing a new age, not the Middle Ages; that the earlier polemic, which was in the true sense of the word fabulous, was now a matter of official protocol and record, controlled by dates, witnesses, and evidence. Now there was due process; now there were rules of order governing examination, proof, and report.

"Peace and order"—on everyone's lips during the period of humanism and Reformation—did indeed mark a significant advance over the *Fehderechte,* the legalized feuds of the previous age. In legislation and politics, in jurisprudence and in administration, what is "modern" about the modern age is clearly perceptible. Even the expulsion of Jews has been wrenched from the spontaneity of public furor. Expulsion can be accomplished only after consideration of the facts, and even then only "from above." As long as the laws of torture, however, were in place, ethnic minorities comprising a "public threat," such as Jews and witches, could be indicted, interrogated, and legally sentenced on grounds of sacrilege, which popular rumor and the educated press might allege, and the torture chamber confirmed.

14

The Jews as Signposts to the Reformation

The question of continuity within Luther's thought on the Jews has absorbed scholarly energies at a growing rate.[24] The preliminary question, to what degree Luther's perceptions are a reflex of the continuity of the age, seems, on the other hand, to be settled. Here, at least, there are no problems and have been none for some time. If Luther was a friend of the Jews, he ruptured the continuity; if a foe of the Jews, then he extended the Middle Ages' lease into the modern era. Plunging unpremeditatedly and indiscriminately into Luther yields just such rough-hewn, anachronistic alternatives. Philo-Semitism does not exist in the sixteenth century, and among the Christians, friends of the Jews are rare exceptions: the title attaches most deservedly to Justus Jonas and Andreas Osiander. But everyone had a hand in the polemic against the Jews.

It pays, then, to fine tune our hearing, and to learn to distinguish degrees of harshness and intensities of slander, levels of argumentation and points of attack. The "proofs" of Mary vilification, desecrations of the host, and child murder—whether submitted by Höltzel or later by Hubmaier, Hätzer, or Eck—all strive to document the Jewish menace. "An Incredible Event" is singularly meaningful for our understanding of Luther because of its contrast value. In the eyes of the printer Hieronymous Höltzel, the Brandenburg affair is no isolated incident to be adjudicated on the merits of the case, but rather a direct outgrowth of a hatred for Christians and the murder of Christ. This is not the case for Luther—in no phase of his work, at no level of his polemic.

If we consider Luther not in the context of his contemporaries but in the context of his posterity, the problems are of an entirely different nature. However nuanced and differentiated, every form of attack and every standpoint taken in the battle against the Jews today draws the apparently illuminating verdict of "anti-Semitism." Historical scholarship becomes ipso facto superfluous once we project the Darwinistic theory of natural selection and the later ideology of racism onto the past, in the belief that from such a presumably elevated watchtower we can at last make sense of history. To resist this temptation, one must realize that Luther does not see "a race" when he looks at the Jews, nor are baptized and unbaptized Jews for Luther the exponents of an ethnic, racial unit. Baptized Jews belong unqualifiedly to the people of God, just as do baptized Germans, the Gentiles.

Consequently, Luther does not regard unbaptized Jews as born murderers or villains; they are the living embodiment of a religion, and in particular, of that legalistic religion adhered to with a vengeance not only by unbaptized Jews. In the course of his Reformation discovery, Luther became convinced that Judaism had attracted an alarmingly large following within the papal church. And later, in the struggle for the reformation of the church, it grew clear to him that Jewish legalism now posed the identical threat to the evangelical church. Over the years, this view of the collision between the religion of law and the gospel, between the record of salvation and the record of calamities, between God and the devil, Christ and the antichrist, remained a constant in Luther's thought. Luther never chanced upon a race theory. Much to the contrary, his ire was provoked by any "ethnic theology" that sought to identify the seed of Abraham with the people of God.

One must select with care the work that will introduce us to Luther's thought. One point of departure could be the late writings on the Jews[25] in which Luther vehemently warned the church against the perils of Jewish infection and launched into polemical tirades against the rabbinical lies and distortions of the Holy Scriptures. But then the early, supposedly sympathetic utterances on the Jews could seem to have been rescinded. In this case, one might conclude that later, personal experiences and Luther's own study of Jewish texts had shattered his youthful dreams of toleration.[26] On the other hand, if one were to start with Luther's indictment of "Christian" conduct toward Jews in the tract dating from 1523, *Jesus Christ was Born a Jew*, one would risk tempering the harshness of the late writings by brushing them aside as symptoms of senility.[27] There is always the danger of idealizing the young Luther, exalting his output of the 1520s as a beacon of freedom and intellectual testament, while comfortably relegating to the shelf the practically unknown late works under the lable, "Relapse Into the Middle Ages."[28]

Another false tack appears so self-evidently correct that we have gradually and uncritically lost all sense of proportion: Restricting the focus to the five writings specifically devoted to "the Jews" not only intolerably depletes the evidence, but actually preprograms it; the fact that the Jewish question is lodged in the bedrock of Luther's theology is on this approach obscured from the very start.[29] For some, the Jewish question then becomes an optional side issue that, although tragic in its consequences, is not Luther's burden, but the burden of his times. Others, for whom the Jewish writings suffice, hit upon the candid question: Martin, what do you think of the Jews?—and find its self-contained answer, too: Luther was not the victim of his times, but the fanatic victimizer. Yet precisely this *Gretchenfrage* deserves patient attention and a complete answer. We shall accordingly begin at what must, in terms of chronology and still more of genre, be described as the "midpoint" of Luther, namely, those writings, which Luther presented as the paradigm of faith and the abbreviated form of confession.

In the first half of 1520, Luther combined two earlier published works—the commentaries on the Ten Commandments (1518) and on the Lord's Prayer (1519)—and inserted between them the interpretation of the apostolic confession of faith. The third article of faith ran as follows: "No Jew, heretic, heathen, or sinner shall be saved without reconciling himself to and embracing the congregation of the faithful."[30] Nine years later, in Luther's Large Catechism, this demarcation of the church of Christ was fortified and enhanced—the Turks are now added to the list[31]—but the clearly recognizable foundation is preserved: belief in a "holy, Christian church" (*sancta ecclesia catholica*) separates "us Christians from all other peoples on earth . . . be they heathens, Turks, Jews, or false Christians and hypocrites."[32]

If the confession is concerned with delineating the church of faith, in gospel preaching the fixing of these boundaries marks off a veritable battleground. In the later sermons, which date from the beginning of the 1530s, Luther called for a mustering of troops under the "captain Christ" to repel the increasingly violent attacks of Satan upon the central tenets of the faith.[33] This inimical campaign against the true church was of course no new theme, either in the ecclesiastical tradition or for the young Luther.[34] Once, however, the gospel had been recovered, formulated in the confession, and laid down as the cornerstone of the evangelical church, Luther experienced the assault upon the true church as it was foretold in the Holy Scriptures: the devil, vexed and provoked in the extreme, was mounting the final, major, that is to say apocalyptic, offensive through his legions of Romans, heretics, Turks, and Jews.

The harsh writings on the Jews—there is no denying it—are uncompromisingly severe. They are not, however, an aberration. They neither constitute an anomalous topic nor are they the manifestation of a neurotic hatred whose origins lie in early childhood experiences or in the shocks incurred in later life. Instead, they are an expression of Luther's assessment of the condition of the church at the close of history. Though the church was always under fire from the devil, this assault assumes a new vehemence with the approach of the world's end. St. Augustine had already pointed this out to the Middle Ages in the great historical work, *The City of God*. Luther now knew that the time had come. The devil would mobilize all his auxiliary forces to beat back the Reformation, all the way back to Rome.

In retrospect, the sequence of Jews, heretics, and apostates is already a fundamental element in the theology of the young Luther.[35] This chain of iniquity is, in the first place, an aid to biblical exegesis; it belongs to the *Instrumentarium*, and as such is useful for uncovering the biblical text's manifold levels of discourse. For it is in the Scriptures, chiefly in the Old Testament, that we find on the level of literal meaning (*sensus literalis*) a description of the great works of God in the past. On the level of interpretation for the Christians of "today," we encounter the existential and dogmatic application of the text, upon which the individual Christian is to base his faith and conduct (*sensus tropologicus*), and the church as a body its confessional dogma and teachings (*sensus allegoricus*). Applied to the Jews, this means that what is said literally of them, namely, that they are obstinate, holds true in an extended, allegorical sense for all "refractory Christians" and refers tropologically or ethically to the stubborn capacity for sin that inheres in man.[36] Note that this correlation is not one of Luther's personal discoveries; he could have found it worked out already in Augustine's commentary on the Psalms[37] as well as in medieval exegetical practice, where it was hammered into a rigid formula.[38]

To Luther, this chain of iniquity—Jews, heretics, and counterchurch—signified more than just an elementary aid to Bible investigation. Grouping together the forces inimical to God gave Luther tremendous powers of hindsight, which allowed him to read the signs of the times and to distinguish the various periods of world history according to the "progress" of unbelief. Unbelief and forgetfulness of God had from the beginning surrounded the church, but under different standard-bearers in every era: the Jews in the time of Christ, the heretics in the time of the church fathers, and lastly and worst of all, "we miserable Christians ourselves."[39] All three ("we miserable Christians" included) had failed throughout the ages to keep the convenant with God, all had consigned his Word and his works to oblivion and thus tempted judgment.[40]

This tripartite division of history, like the chain of iniquity, was a traditional given. For Augustine, the first period of church history was that of the persecution of Christians; the second, his own time, of the heretics and the false Christians; the third period would arrive when the antichrist—in the church, easily confused with Christ; in the world, vastly superior to him—had assembled all the threats of the previous ages and dashed them down upon Christianity.[41] In the Middle Ages, Augustine provided Bernard of Clairvaux (d. 1153) with material for a reevaluation and reinterpretation that was strikingly new, based as it was on prophecy of inner evil. The early church had endured under persecution by the heathen; until the eleventh century, the fathers managed to defend the ecclesiastical walls against the external assault of the heretics; but at present, in the third and final period, the age of dissolution from within had arrived.[42]

In Luther, these two strands come together—scriptural understanding and historical interpretation, the diabolical chain of iniquity and the step-by-step approach of the antichrist, who in the end of days will undermine and infiltrate the church of Christ as never before. The Jews are no longer simply archaeological precursors in the history of the gospel's fulfillment; they serve as precise coordinates for charting evil's invasion of the church in Luther's own day. Luther's image of the Jews does not darken with rage because they are desecrators of the sacraments, child murderers or usurers, and least of all on account of their ethnic or racial singularity. The critical issue is that the Jews are a prototypical "compass" for determining the devil's points of penetration into the contemporary church. Not "the Jew" but "the Jews" are the coordinates in this search.

Luther's first major lecture series as a young professor in Wittenberg from 1513 to 1515 was devoted to the Psalms. Already here this surveyor's tool is implemented at every step; whatever is said of the Jews applies equally to the heretics, and at the same time exposes the aberrancies of the contemporary church, both in its dogma and its practice. The first two links, Jews and heretics, function as fixed constants that provide the intepreter with a framework for the application to his own time, relative to the textual and contextual requirements of the particular Psalm verse under consideration.

Over the years, ascertain in his readings of the Psalms and in increasing measure even in his readings of the Hebraic originals, Luther strove to ascertain the course of the church, past and present. Psalm after psalm is followed by observation upon observation; textual exegesis turns into contemporary diagnosis; the focus shifts from the Jews of the ancient past to us Jews today.

That Mohammed allies himself with the Jews and threatens the church from without is not surprising. But the sharp menacing tip is already implanted deep within: the church is contaminated to the core with false teachers, feuding universities, and monastic orders that chase after their own honor. We miserable Christians are ourselves today's most conspicuous Jews. This is no humble, private confession or pious self-accusation; at stake is not moral conduct or profligate dissolution, but truth or lies. Without the correct dogma, we shall fall victim to the original malediction and to the world, ruled by pride and excessive self-confidence, open to superstition, closed to belief, self-righteously and arrogantly becoming a law unto ourselves.[43]

This final diagnosis, arrived at with the help of his "Jew-detector," is the most common one in Luther; it is, so to speak, a bundling of all the single diagnoses into one. The "righteous" are swerving from the right faith[44] since they will not submit to the judgment of God, to the Scriptures, or to the testimony of the church fathers. The strong will to withstand God is the source of contagion for a multitude of life-threatening diseases that can now be identified. The Jews are a clear example of how clinging fast to one's own righteousness leads to contradition, resistance, and finally to rebellion against God.[45] Luther's line of sight extends far beyond Golgotha, beyond the place of crucifixion, and reaches into the church of his own day. Today we are crucifying Christ anew.

The Jews likewise afford an insight into what will soon be at stake in the open battle for grace and faith: impious self-righteousness boils down to unredeemable atheism. He who is righteous by his own rights is not prepared to acknowledge God or to let God be God.[46]

In Luther's judgment of the Jews, a third fact becomes obvious: the wrath of God will punish the faithlessness of his people. If we refuse to turn to God, we shall be smitten by God's hand.[47] Just as God punished the people of Israel with the Babylonian captivity and with "misery" until now, so will he deal with the Christian people. Here, the Jews are driving the loyal son of Rome, the young professor Martin Luther, for the first time to the borders of an unheard-of suspicion: are we miserable Christians not already in exile?

There is no about-face in Luther's thinking when, in August of 1514, prompted by the conversionist offensive of the theological circle of Cologne that was centered in the baptized Jew Johannes Pfefferkorn, Luther spoke out against the burning of Jewish books. The Jews cannot be converted through such purges, with fire and the sword. They know as little about what it means to stand well before the Lord as do Christians. This being the case, we should instead see in them our own reflection, and ourselves fear the wrath of God.[48] Before the young Luther openly entered—or even could enter—the lists for Reformation, he began to understand something about the Jews: the wrath of God applies to all, Jews and Christians alike, all those who oppose his Word. Luther does not upgrade the Jews; he indicts the Christians.

15

Jews and Christians
in Exile

The grouping of "Jews, heretics, and pseudo-Christians"—by which is meant not lukewarm "Good Friday Christians," but the devil's fifth column—remains a constant in Luther's theology, from the early writings to the late. All three are the devil's drudges, posed against the true Israel, against the everlasting church of faith.[49] In October of 1518, the papal legate Cardinal Cajetan conducted hearings with the already notorious critic of indulgences and insisted on a flat recantation. At this point, Luther's hope that the papal church would be able and willing to move toward reform vanished into thin air. Increasingly it became difficult to allay the dreadful suspicion that the antichrist had already usurped the Holy See in Rome. Together with his age, Luther knew that with the unleashing of the antichrist, the last phase of secular history had dawned. The presence of the kingdom of Satan, felt in all periods, was in the final phase of history intensifed to a new degree; the devil's burst into the open had achieved an unknown vehemence.

Tense and expectant, the young Luther scanned the horizon for signs of the world's end; he knew exactly where to look and what to look for. From the first detection of symptoms in 1520, the Jews supplied Luther with the hard data and diagnostic equipment he needed for monitoring the Christian sickness unto death.[50] Page after page the Jews remained for Luther the key to the interpretation of the age—after the close of his Old Testament lecture on the Psalms, in his work on the New Testament, his great lecture series on Paul (1515–18). Prior to 1520 Luther saw his times besieged but not yet overrun by the antichrist: the Jews, who stand under God's bane not merely in their hidden spiritual darkness but before the eye of the world as well, are God's way of publicly manifesting the real condition of the entire church.[51] In this early phase, before suffering excommunication and the imperial ban (1521), Luther was not interested in the contemporary Jews. His worry was the church, critically endangered by its forgetfulness of God; the church as reflected in the history of the Jewish legalistic religion and in its contemporary presence. The Christians of today are similar to Jews and, indeed, much worse (*immo peiores*).[52]

Without ever losing sight of the exemplary, diagnostic, and deterrent function of the Jews,[53] in the Wittenberg years of public proclamation of the gospel from both pulpit and study, Luther underscored the misery of the shared fate and shared blindness: the evangelical proclamation is the last chance for conversion for disoriented Jews and Christians alike. After the "calculations" reported in the lectures of the early phase (before 1520) were incorporated into an unambiguous image, and once the disparate observations in the "Jews' Mirror" had yielded a foolproof identification of the false church,[54] the Babylonian captivity of the Jews was discovered to be a prison-house for Jews and Christians alike.[55] No cleansing operation, no Inquisition, no pious pope, and no progressive, reforming general council were of any use at this stage. Only God could still save and extricate: reformation was God's business, not the work of man.[56]

The apparently sympathetic pronouncements of Luther on the Jews can now be appreciated for what they are worth: "If hatred for the Jews, heretics, and Turks makes one a Christian, then we, with all our rage, make the very best of Christians. If, on the other hand, love for Christ is the decisive factor, then we are doubtless worse than all the Jews, heretics, and Turks put together."[57] Whereas a similar pronouncement gained Erasmus undeserved credit for supporting toleration of Jews, but here Luther is rashly charged with a reversal in position. Luther's remark, however, does not signal a transformation in his thinking or a sudden valorization of Jews that goes hand in hand with the "Reformation breakthrough." Instead, Luther decries the hate-engendering contamination disseminated by ecclesiastical bearers of the "Jewish" plague (*participes impietatis Judaicae*).[58]

The proclamation of the gospel had exposed the devil's invasion of the church and confronted his enslavement of men with the counterweapon, the freedom of God's grace. At this critical stage, the devil has no choice but to defend himself with all his forces. He is provoked to the limit[59] and is massing his great coalition of Jews, Turks, and pope. Through rebels and fanatics he is even able to press the newly discovered gospel into his own service and thus thwart the Reformation by treachery. Here the Jews relinquish their function as mirror and "detector." They now threaten, with their presence and numbers—as always, in league with all the enemies of God—to herd the emancipated people back into captivity. In the climax of the world's end, the Jews widen their warfare from the church to the emperor and empire, but again only as the satellites and emissaries of the apocalyptic incarnation of evil. The many—Jews, Turks, pope—now comprise one single assailant.

Once more back to the beginnings. The writings that emerged from Luther's struggle over the correct understanding of the Bible in the years after 1513 are consistent in their judgment of the counterchurch; its fundamental constituents include, besides the Jews, heretics and pseudo-Christians. The consequences of this grouping are considerable and materialize as three steps of a single progression of thought.

First, the repudiation of Christ by the Jews is being repeated inside today's own church. In its insistence upon self-righteousness, the *Sautheologie*[60] ("sow-theology") of the present day contradicts and resists the coming of God in Christ.

Second, in reflecting on the Jews' claim that as the seed of Abraham they collectively constitute the people of God forever Luther discovers the groundlessness of the parallel claim: whoever adheres to the pope adheres to Christ—*ubi papa, ibi ecclesia*. Papal obedience and the consensus of the ruling church as little ensure truth and salvation as does kinship with Abraham.[61] A child of God does not put faith in kinship and works, but solely in God's twofold gift of grace and the community of faith. God not only redeems sinners, he gathers them into the visible church of the Word—*ubi verbum, ibi ecclesia*, "whoever adheres to the Word adheres to Christ."

The evangelical doctrine of justification in conjunction with a new understanding of the church now leads to a third consequence. Access to the gospel is no longer blocked; the time for Jewish conversion has arrived. Only when viewed in isolation can this expectation be construed as a radical turn. Luther did not, however, foresee any comprehensive Jewish conversion, and his hope was in no way restricted to the Jews alone. It is the true church, composed of Jews and Gentiles, that will be set free and led home from its captivity—this is Luther's message to his students as early as the lectures on the Epistle to the Romans (1515/16), when in the winter of 1516 he abandons his brief written text and works out the implications of his insight extempore.[62]

From 1519 to 1523, Luther was driven by one thought: God is at work and has begun to wrest his people—Jews and Gentiles—from their Babylonian captivity. Thanks to the rediscovery of the gospel,

Christ can now be proclaimed distortion-free.[63] In this way will the faith that is the sole hope for the true church be roused.[64] Luther was not at all seized with a sudden optimism about fresh prospects for conversion, such as could be explained by encouraging experiences with Jews in the Wittenberg circle or at the Diet of Worms in 1521.[65]

The provocative title of his work from 1523, *Jesus Christ Was Born a Jew*, is readily adduced today to soften the features of the supposedly malicious old Luther through reference to the (supposedly otherwise) young Luther. Yet Luther's critique of Judaism as a religion is just as uncompromising in 1523 as it is in the later years: Christianity and Judaism are mutually exclusive; Reformation does not imply salvation for Jews. Nor does Luther reckon on the likelihood that Jews will rush in droves to their conversion, as several evangelical pietists, Puritans, and even orthodox Lutherans would later assume. As a community, Jews—like Turks, heretics, and false Christians—stand under the aegis of the antichrist. Access to the Word should, however, be made available to the "remnant," whose preservation was foreseen by the prophet Isaiah (10:20–22). Despite the intractability of the great majority, says Luther in his own hymn to faith, his explication of the hymn of praise to Mary (*Magnificat*, 1520/21), we should not treat the Jews in an unfriendly manner, "for there are still future Christians among them. . . ."[66]

This is not a special-case theology for Jews. The same principles hold for all of God's enemies, for pseudo-Christians and non-Christians, for Turks and papists: the boundaries of the church are far from having been disclosed definitively to our eyes. There are those among the enemy ranks, outside or inside the church, who have never heard the gospel. God has granted an adjournment of the tribunal—just this once. The children of God can never be congregated through excommunication or inquisition. Heretics will be overcome not by fire at the stake but by the fire of love.[67] We can convert the Turks, as we can our own "bigwigs" in the church and state, only through persuasion, not through force.[68]

When in defiance of both imperial banishment and ecclesiastical excommunication Luther came out of hiding at the Wartburg and hurried back to Wittenberg, he did not check the Reformation in Wittenberg out of sympathy for the pope, or with political calculations in mind. For a week long he defended himself with trenchant eloquence from the pulpit of the Wittenberg castle church, and there delivered his so-called *Seven Sermons* against the formalization of the Reformation by government resolution and enactment of law. The *Altgläubige*—the "old believers," the unreformed orthodoxy—have to be won over through the Word; therefore: "Forbearance with the weak!" This apparent instance of singular behavior is not something that can only be accounted for by the confused and precarious state of affairs in Wittenberg. "Forbearance with the weak" is in fact an organic component of a unified vision: there are still Christians among "them"![69]

16

The Harshness
of the Old Luther

With the proclamation of the gospel, Jews and Christians are discovered to be in the same condition, if not in the same camp, companions in misery and in exile. What became of this solidarity along the way such that the old Luther could affirm: "Everything concurs with Christ's judgment that the Jews are venomous, bitter, vengeful, slimy snakes, assassins and devil's children, who steal and wreak havoc on the sly because they cannot afford to do so in the open. A Christian has, next to the devil, no more venomous, bitter enemy than the Jew." Is the thesis of Luther's reversal accurate after all? Does the pat formula about the "hardening and narrowing in the course of the years" prove to be in fact an understated, cosmetic gloss for the radical collapse of Luther's earlier ideals? Does Luther ultimately despair of forbearance with the weak when, in February 1546, he closes his final sermon with this testament: The Jews ought to convert, "but if they refuse, we should neither tolerate nor suffer their presence in our midst!"[70]

To judge correctly we must recognize from the outset that Luther did not link the Reformation to an expectation of better times; he was not preparing for the future coexistence of all men and races. As creatures of modernity, we instinctively evaluate the Reformation according to the Enlightenment standards of religious, social, and political emancipation; by such criteria, Luther did advance beyond the Middle Ages. Yet the principles of his faith and the mainspring of his program are not those of that later vision of continuous progress and improvement: Reformation was a "grace period" and a postponement, not the beginning of a new age but the end of time as we know it. This end, in Luther's eyes, passed through three phases: before, during, and after the first public proclamation of the rediscovered gospel—in the pre-Reformation, the Reformation, and the successful Counter-Reformation.

From 1519/20, the young Luther publicly proclaimed his gospel discovery and propagated it in the popular idiom. The next stage involved the organization of the congregation through catechism and confession, through liturgical and institutional reform (1523–29). In time, the congregation took on a visible shape: it was the assemblage of believers, the evangelical church against which now, in the final phase of secular history, all opposing powers were consolidated. The Counter-Reformation siege had set in as expected. All attacks of the earlier phases were concentrated at the end of time. Christian persecutions rivaling those under the Roman Empire were conducted with a renewed horror, both in Germany throughout many of its territories and in the whole of Europe, from the Netherlands to Spain and Italy. The massive onslaught of the heretics, met in the past by the frontline fathers and teachers of the church, now imperiled the constancy of faith on all flanks. Once again the central teachings about God and Christ were in jeopardy. What is more, the prophecy of Bernard of Clairvaux was coming to fulfillment in the age of Reformation in the church: at the end of time, Christ's flock would experience its greatest threat from within its own ranks. It was for this reason that Luther reacted so savagely against dissidents within the evangelical camp, whether against his colleague in Wittenberg, Andreas Karlstadt, or against the Zurich reformer Huldreich Zwingli.

A characteristic feature of the old Luther up to his death was his unflagging exertions against this concert of diabolical attacks on all fronts at once. The first tactic he prescribed was to use the red cape of the gospel to provoke the hidden emissaries of the devil into the open and then to withstand with all one's might the shock of their stampede. In 1537, in the middle of the last period of his life, Luther captured in a single sentence the gravity of the church's peril, and simultaneously the confidence with which it could face the battle: "And this is a sorely needed consolation for the Christians, namely, that they ought not doubt that the Christian church will remain in the world, amid all the infidels, the Turks, the heathen, the Jews, the heretics, and the rabble, beside the very devil himself and his angels. For here is written the prophecy that neither lies nor fails: the Holy Ghost 'shall teach you all things, and bring all things to your remembrance'" (John 14:26).[71]

That the Reformation would have to reckon with resistance; that the Reformation would moreover not weaken but instead actually strengthen the opposition was, for Luther, a certainty and an expected consequence of the apocalypse. He had only to scan the signs of the times to recognize that the number of days remaining was rapidly declining. Which events became a sign for him, always with the proviso that God's calendar is beyond human reckoning? Luther's literary output, collected in one hundred solid volumes including a profusion of extremely personal remarks in letters and "table talks" (*Tischreden*), permits a fully documented examination of his life in its various stages. In this way it is possible to reconstruct the pattern of events and experiences that Luther linked to the escalation toward the final collision.

First, there were the shocks registered within the most intimate sphere. The psychohistorian who traces outward behavior back to psychological processes will want to point out Luther's loss of his father in 1530. Plunged into deep grief at the news that his father Hans had died on May 29, he wrote straightaway to Melanchthon: "Now I assume the inheritance of our name; I am indeed the senior Luther in my family."[72] By inheritance Luther did not mean material bequest, but the right to succeed his father as the next in line "into death and on to Christ."[73]

Far more significant than Luther's psychic profile, the much belabored symptoms of the eccentricities of old age, or even of encroaching senile regression, was the anxiety and grief that the cause of the gospel in his own country brought him. This was the root of his undeniable intransigence: Germany is once again on the brink of forgetting how miserable the captivity in fact is from which God is at work rescuing his people.[74] The gospel of freedom is degenerating into a license for despising the common good. The Peasants' War is not the only example; princes are turning the gospel into a political bargaining chip, and the evangelical theologians would have us believe that they are more clever than the Scriptures. The expected Counter-Reformation has clearly set in, and every striking success of the devil has been just as strikingly foreseen by faith.

Next Luther produces one account after another describing his "Reformation breakthrough," summarized in classic form in 1545. The aim was to mobilize the unsuspecting youth and to reveal the darkness looming about them which, not yet entirely overcome, threatened once more to engulf the world. In "table talks" and lectures, Luther suddenly becomes preoccupied again with his spiritual father Johannes von Staupitz, a topic Luther had consigned to silence ever since Staupitz's death in 1524.[75] When Luther now breaks silence, it is not on the assumption that the memory of his spiritual father will fill the void left by the death of his natural father. As Staupitz had once done, so now does Luther himself take a stand on the front line. Thus does his autobiography become a testament, and the testament the final battle cry against the archenemy of Christ. Seen from Luther's perspective as well as from our own, this testament can mean only one thing: the Reformation lies not in the past but in the future; the release from the Babylonian captivity is not completed, but underway.

In the wider sphere of public events, Luther's attentions were likewise focused upon the time around 1530. Looking back, he interpreted the roll call at the Augsburg Confession before the emperor and Diet on 22 June 1530 as the final and most critical opportunity for rapprochement between the two sides in the battle for the renewal of the church. From the denouncement of the confession onward (officially from 3 August 1530) the distance between the papal church and the gospel had become a definitive rupture.[76] At the end of 1518 Luther had suspected the workings of the antichrist in the papacy;[77] he now stepped up his attacks to the level of a heavy barrage "against the papacy in Rome, which is underwritten by the devil."[78] Later that same year (1545), Luther restated his position with graphic crudity in his unvarnished commentary to Lucas Cranach's equally heavy-handed, satirical images. Thus, for instance, we find the pope depicted in the jaws of hell, crowned by his cohorts, the brood of Satan. Luther's rhyme supplied the commentary to this picture.

> In the devil's name here sits
> The holy pope, palpable at last;
> That he is the very antichrist
> is proclaimed in Holy Writ.[79]

Luther's reaction to the threat to the empire posed by the militant advance of Islam was no less extreme. Between 1519 and 1529, he had already begun to label the Turks "the devil's helpmates": they are an infernal, destructive power; not the outcome of blind destiny, but the very scourge of God. The response of the church must accordingly be other than that of the secular authorities. For this reason, Luther could reject a religious crusade while still insisting on the legitimacy of a war of defense.[80] When the imperial Diet convened in Augsburg, Luther was compelled to remain behind at the most southerly fortress of electoral Saxony, in the Franconian Coburg. In his isolation at this stronghold, he began, in April 1530, to translate and explicate Ezekiel 38 and 39: the monsters depicted here, Gog and Magog, are two superpowers joined in battle against the people of God. Interpreted in the late Middle Ages as a reference

to the Jews,[81] on Luther's reading the two infernal powers stand for the Turks.[82] Once the devil sees that the pope, emperor, king, and princes lack the power to stem the gospel, "he conceives the idea of annihilating it by force through his Gog."[83] While Melanchthon is wringing his hands over the waning hopes for peace and tending to the political problems of the empire at the Diet in Augsburg, he himself, Luther writes during these days of the summer of 1530, is focusing on the kingdom of Satan, which seeks to devour both body *and* soul: "Now I am beginning to direct myself and all my powers against the Turks and Mohammed. . . ."[84]

Luther now turns against the pope and the Turks with a hitherto unparalleled rage and ferocity. The two entities are of a piece, and together constitute a monstrous giant: the pope is the spirit and the Turk is the flesh of the antichrist.[85] But soon a third rushes to join with his fellows in the diabolical alliance: the already familiar precursor in the gallery of ancestors of gospel opponents—the unconverted, indeed, the flagrantly unconvertible Jew. Jews, Turks, and the pope were from the very beginning the storm troops of the devil's forces. Long on military alert within the theological framework, they are now an army palpably at hand.

Our pursuit of Luther's alleged about-face from solidarity to Jew-baiting was prompted by an original question. An answer is now feasible. Solidarity with the antichrist was for Luther—as it was for his age—unthinkable at any time, as much in 1523 as in 1546. Equally nonproblematic at any time for Luther was the grouping together of Jews, Turks, and pseudo-Christians. "Luther and the Jews" thus becomes a separate issue only in virtue of the historical developments that postdate Luther. It is true that Luther's portfolio included works on the Jews, but these, along with the writings against the pope and the Turks, belong to a single, indissoluble generic category: apolcalyptic prophecy. It is possible to extract relevant quotations from the late works, that is, the testimony from the years 1530–46; there is no shortage of anti-Jewish remarks, and each one taken alone is shocking enough. But they can be read as Jew-baiting material and added to the arsenal of evidence for Luther's anti-Semitism only if, from the distant vantage point of our own times, we ingenuously ignore his bracketing together of anti-Jewish writings and apocalyptic expectation. In sum, racial antagonism has as little to do with the old Luther as solidarity has to do with the young. For subsequent history that means: Jewish obstinacy retards the coming end as little as Jewish conversion hastens it. For Luther, a "Jew-free" Germany will never lead to the millennial kingdom.

17

The Jews
at the End of Time

What triggered the Jews' transformation from precursor into pro-
tagonist of evil cannot be pinned down with absolute certainty. Clear
in any case is that the conspiracy of all the devil's forces in the last
days, a tradition firmly established through centuries of consensus,
also comprised the Jews as an element in the threat-potential of the
apocalyptic end. Having tracked the antichrist to Rome, in the 1530s
Luther pondered over the alliance of the Jews with the Turks. During
this time, moreover, while the quarrel with the Anabaptists was
worsening, the suspicion arose in all quarters that the Anabaptists
were so thoroughly contaminated by Judaism that they now denied
the validity of the sacraments of the New Testament—Holy Baptism
and the Eucharist. Their blasphemy against Christ in the sacraments
was for Luther as grievous as the Jews' "perennial" blasphemy
against Christ in the flesh: the fanatical revilers of the sacrament are
for all practical purposes indistinguishable from the Jews. The devil
"fills the crazed masses with such splendid blasphemies as this: that
our sacrament is nothing but gobbling up meat and swilling down
blood. . . . The Jews in our day do no differently; to bind their
children to their faith, they blaspheme Christianity horribly. . . ."[86]
   As rumors thickened in the 1530s to the effect that Christians in
large stretches of Europe, from Bohemia and Moravia to Poland,
were having themselves circumcised[87] and were thronging to adopt
Jewish ritual,[88] Luther's determination to take public action against
this "apostasy and lapse" was brewing. The outcome was *Against
the Sabbatarians* (1538), a work that today is still numbered among
the anti-Jewish writings, although its argument is in fact aimed at
winning back the newly made Jews. Judaism has no future, it is dead
history: "The Jews are now fifteen hundred years out of Jerusalem
and in misery; they have neither temple, service, priesthood, nor

princedom. And thus has their law lain buried in ashes for as many years, along with Jerusalem and the Jewish kingdom."[89]

However greatly Christian despisers of the sacraments may resemble the Jews, we learn in a table talk from the first half of the 1530s, they have to be handled with discrimination. To the question of whether the sacramentarians ought not to be tolerated like the Jews, Luther replies: Jews are patent blasphemers. Therefore, they are shunned and accordingly can do no damage. What is more, they do not wish to establish their own authority and church. "For these reasons, they can be tolerated."[90] In other words, toleration for non-Christian religions is permissible provided such religions conduct no missions and observe the law of the land. The sacramentarians, on the other hand, unlike the Jews, insinuate themselves into the church and at the same time refuse to submit to its authority. Luther then lays down the axiom that defines the limits of toleration and forms the basis of the Jewish policy he will advocate in his final years: "But if anyone whosoever, *sive Iudaeus sive christianus*, be he Jew or Christian, should wish to hold the office of a preacher or an emperor, *non est ferendum hoc*—that cannot be tolerated."[91]

The fanatics do not mark the only place of penetration. As before, but now to an even greater degree, the threat posed by the Turks is directly connected with the Jewish danger. The advance of the Turks upon Germany shocked Luther more profoundly than any other occurrence. Unlike the Curia in Rome, however, he did not summon Christianity to a crusade; there was more at stake than the kingdom of the emperor.[92] The waves of war have always swept over the earth. Kingdoms come and go by, rise and fall—this is not new; it is the way of the world. But soon there will be no more world. The frightful end is close, the earth is degenerate, and the vessel of God's wrath will empty onto a godless world, as the last book of the Bible foretells (Rev. 16:1).[93]

As word reached Luther that the siege of Vienna had lifted on 18 October 1529, he saw this turn of events not as a disproof, but as a grace period. Time was running out, the devils were raging, as was to be expected in the Last Days.[94] In his analysis of the siege, an explanation for the scope and severity of national imperilment crops up apparently on the side: Germany is infested with traitors who support the Turks[95]—a suspicion that in the language of the day was a common gloss for the Jews. Johannes Pfefferkorn, who was one who "ought to know," certified that the Jews were expecting the end of their misery to come from no other source "than through the destruction of the Holy Roman Empire."[96] Luther, however, did not need this conspiracy theory. Jews and Turks were allied through bonds far more potent than military tactics and political calculation.

After Elector John Frederick (1532–46) issued an expulsion mandate for Saxony's Jews in August 1536,[97] Josel of Rosheim, recognized far beyond his Alsatian homeland as the "ruler of German Jewry," attempted to intervene through Luther, who it was hoped, would be able to win over the elector. The contract was drawn up by the Strasbourg reformer Wolfgang Capito, hardly a pro-Jewish sympathizer but rather, like his teacher Reuchlin, a Christian Hebraist full of respect for Jewish erudition.[98] Luther's refusal of aid to Josel is often read as the point of no return in his progression toward hostility to the Jews. But Luther stressed that he had always been and still was convinced that Jews ought to be treated "in a friendly manner" to ensure that no obstacles stood in the way of their conversion by God. Luther held firm to this belief to the very end, even if this amiability turned into a "severe mercy."

Protection of Jews was not his job, Luther insisted. It was a matter for the civil authorities who were responsible for the general well-being of the state. Reuchlin's famous dictum on the Jews is the most apposite: If the Jews do not show signs of improvement, they must be expelled—*"reformandi seu expellendi."*[99] The Jews were in Luther's eyes far removed from any state of perfection; if anything, they had gotten "worse," obviously through his own encouragement: they blaspheme and curse the name of Jesus of Nazareth; they hold Christians to be their "chiefest enemies"; so deeply does their hatred run that "if you could, you would ravage the Christians in every respect, what they are and what they own." But the decision not to intervene on behalf of the Jews in Saxony hinged on Luther's reasoned belief that, while on the surface, the Jews were struggling to improve their lot, in actual fact they were grappling for nothing other than their past. Nothing, however, could reverse the misery of the Jewish exile. There remained only to "accept your kinsman and Lord, the beloved, crucified Jesus Christ, as we Gentiles have done." Luther's intercession for the Jews as the "kinsmen of Jesus" must not deepen their entrenchment as the opponents of Christ. "Kindly take this friendly advice . . . since, for the sake of the crucified Jew, whom none can take away from me, I would readily do what is best for you Jews, unless you should use my good will to further your obstinacy. You know exactly what I mean."[100]

Three days prior to his death, Luther appended to his last sermon (15 February 1546) the tract *An Admonition Against the Jews*, in which both viewpoints are once again blended into a single perspective: Jews are our open enemies. They do not desist from blaspheming our Lord Christ. They call the Virgin Mary a whore, and Christ a whoreson. "And if they could kill us all, they would fain do it, and often do so too."[101] And yet, "we ought to practice Christian love toward them and beg them to convert. . . ."[102]

A third viewpoint, however, is new. If in his letter to Josel, Luther urged the Jewish leader to convert, now he urges the Christian authorities no longer to incur the wrath of God on account of the Jewish presence. What has changed is thus the Jewish policy Luther chooses to endorse, not, however, his view of the Jews as links in the chain "Jews, pope, and Turks," the three, newly unleashed terrors of the apocalyptic end: Christian authorities, do "not make yourselves party to the sins of others. Beseech God that he be merciful to you and that he preserve your government. That is enough." The Jews should convert, "but if they refuse, we should neither tolerate nor suffer their presence in our midst."[103] This is not an appeal to the rabble that they lay their hands on the Jews, but an unambiguous demand put to the authorities, princes, and nobles[104] that they relinquish their avaricious, self-serving Jewish policies—a theme, moreover, that can be traced back to the programs for social reform we find in pre-Reformation pamphlets. The insistence upon Jewish toleration, to be sure a toleration only in the sense of a coexistence strictly predicated upon conversion, remains a lifelong concern for Luther. The approach of the last days has, however, set a further restriction on the limits of toleration: the grace period is running out.

The "sins of others" which the civil authorities should not tolerate undoubtedly refers to such alleged legal infractions of the Jews[105] as had been freshly circulated by Hieronymus Höltzel[106] on the eve of the Reformation and later by Johannes Eck in 1541.[107] In his harshest pamphlet, *Concerning the Jews and Their Lies* (1543), Luther did nothing to defuse apprehensions about the criminal behavior of the Jews.[108] The harshness of this work does not, however, reside in warnings against the possible future crimes of individual persons, but in its unyielding stance toward Judaism as a whole, which Luther perceived as threatening Christians not with misdeeds, but with falsehoods. This was why Luther had counseled the authorities to burn down the Jewish schools of deceit, the synagogues, to confiscate the rabbinical texts, or—if none of these measures helped—to expel those Jews who refused to convert.[109] The Jewish blasphemies were beginning to bear evil fruits, which made protective measures for Christianity a necessity.

But there is another, and for Luther surely central, dimension to "sins of others," namely, the denial of Christ, which was hardly peculiar to the Jews, but a frequent phenomenon encouraged by the antichrist through his accessories, the pope and the Curia: "I am no longer astonished at the blindness, refractoriness, or evil of the Turks or the Jews, when I look upon the most holy fathers of the church, the popes, cardinals, and bishops, who exhibit the very same qualities. O you terrible anger and incomprehensible tribunal of Divine Majesty. . . ."[110] Luther had long before detected this intimate collusion without ever appealing for expulsion. With the approach of the antichrist, he now has no choice but to effect the final breach—but not only from the Jews! As the days of the world incline to their end, the mind of the old Luther turns not to a crusade against the Turks, nor to hatred of Rome or the Jews, but to keeping the gospel afloat in the world's last ravaged hour.

18

The Jew and
"We Wicked Christians"

The appalling historical drama of the relationship between Christians and Jews confronts us in concentrated form in this single man's
development. Luther's point of departure as a reformer was the Jews,
and specifically, his contemplation of Israel as the people of God and
the deniers of Christ. In the resistance to the Reformation and the
rediscovered gospel, Luther saw a stubbornly maintained apostasy
from God,[111] and behind everything, the reeruptive alliance of all the
powers inimical to God. Even as late as the pamphlet *Concerning the
Jews and Their Lies* (1543), summarized again in his last admonition
(1546), Luther continues to endorse that form of toleration which
leaves room for conversion. But anticipation of the looming last
tribunal[112] lets Luther read and calculate "the signs of the times"[113]
in such a way that the extent of toleration is narrowed to a minimum,
to the very last chance before expulsion. As for the political and
social status of the Jews, Luther's Reformation brought no improvements.

Be that as it may, Luther did not, even in the last period of his life,
adopt that medieval view of the Jews which, at the time of the early
Reformation, was still markedly in evidence in the edict issued by the
bishop of Speyer (1519),[114] and which in the same year led to the
expulsions in Regensburg and Rothenburg ob der Tauber.[115] Luther
advanced beyond the medieval view in two important respects. First,
there was the effect of his impetus on his own circle. It would be a
mistake to identify the Reformation with the person of Luther and to
overlook the long line of significant and often strikingly independent
Luther disciples. The Jewish perspective of Justas Jonas and Andreas
Osiander did not focus on the apocalyptic struggle with the antichrist
and his legions.[116] Their evangelical hope lay in a common millennial
future for Jews and Christians, a liberation at the end of time.[117]

Second, it was not the late-Reformation song material of a Paul Gerhardt (d. 1676) or a Jacob Revius (d. 1658) that coined the formula, "It was not the Jews, Lord Jesus, who crucified you."[118] Already the Wittenberg songbook of 1544 contained a stanza so closely reminiscent of the wording of Luther's own writings and sermons from over the years that, although never explicitly attributed to Luther,[119] it deserves to be deemed genuine Luther material:

> Our heinous crime and weighty sin
> Nailed Jesus to the cross, God's true Son.
> Therefore, we should not in bitterness scold
> You, poor Judas, or the Jewish host.
> The guilt is our own.[120]

The timeless alliance of Jews, heretics, and "us wicked Christians"[121] had, in the tribulations of the world's end, provoked Luther into radical opposition. This historical view of things was equally suited,[122] however, to tapping the deep-rooted, hate-engendering piety of the Passion,[123] which for centuries had turned Holy Week into a time of dreaded horror for the Jews in Christian Europe.[124]

The solidarity in sins shared by "us wicked Christians" and the Jews loses its penitential and reformational force when "Reformation" comes to be understood as the *achieved* exodus from Babylonian captivity. This Protestant triumphalism leaves behind heretics, popes, Jews, and "us wicked Christians" in the landscape of a past that has been overcome. Then Luther's "Jew-detector," the prophetic instrument put in the service of the Reformation struggle for a church on the brink of collapse, is no longer safe from being co-opted into a racialistic solution. Through the Jews, Martin Luther exposed a Christian disposition to collaborate with the incarnation of all evil, the enemy of heaven and earth. The elimination of this shocking perception of Christians led to a devastating view of the Jews. Only through a suppression of this theological foundation could the anti-Judaism inherent in Luther—and in the Christian faith as a whole —become the plaything of modern anti-Semitism. This has happened.

Notes to Part Three

1. See, for example, William L. Shirer, *Aufstieg und Fall des Dritten Reichs* (Cologne, 1961), 232. The following passage is significantly edited from the German translation: "It is difficult to understand the behavior of most German Protestants in the first Nazi years unless one is aware of two things: their history and the influence of Martin Luther. The great founder of Protestantism was both a passionate anti-Semite and a ferocious believer in absolute obedience to political authority. He wanted Germany rid of the Jews and when they were sent away he advised that they be deprived of 'all their cash and jewels and silver and gold' and, furthermore, 'that their synagogues or schools be set on fire, that their houses be broken up and destroyed . . . and they be put under a roof or stable, like the gypsies . . . in misery and captivity as they incessantly lament and complain to God about us' . . . Luther employed a coarseness and brutality of language unequaled in German history until the Nazi time" (*The Rise and Fall of the Third Reich: A History of Nazi Germany* [New York: Simon & Schuster, 1960], 236). Karlheinz Deschner, one year later, is even less reserved: ". . . in the later years, Luther became a raving anti-Semite . . . and Hitler brought anti-Semitism to a grisly perfection" (*Abermals krähte der Hahn. Eine Demaskierung des Christentums von den Evangelisten bis zu den Faschisten*, 3d ed. [Hamburg, 1972; 1st ed., 1962], 457f.). Just how speculative and very likely beholden to the Nazi propaganda this shibboleth is, is made clear by the lamentations within the Nazi camp about the forgotten Luther: "It is an intolerable state of affairs that this manifesto of the great Reformer [*On the Jews and Their Lies*], which is both an important outburst of national religious sentiment and utterly relevant to the present day, is known among practically all Germans, but by name alone, and read only by a very few" (*Luthers Kampfschriften gegen das Judentum*, ed. W. Linden [Berlin, 1936], 7).

2. Yosef Hayim Yerushalmi, *The Lisbon Massacre of 1506 and the Royal Image in the Shebet Yehuda* (Cincinnati: Hebrew Union College—Jewish Institute of Religion, 1976), 6–34. See further, the second volume of the *Geschichte des jüdischen Volkes: Vom 7. bis zum 17. Jahrhundert. Das Mittelalter*, ed. H. H. Ben-Sasson (München, 1979), esp. 276–332.

3. "Sed magis credendum foret exordium calamitatis eorum fuisse magnam et infinitam peccuniam eorum, quam barones cum militibus, cives cum

rusticis ipsis solvere tenebantur. Deo autem gratias semper, qui civitatem Erffurdensem populumque Christianum ibidem inter tot incendia tantaque homicidia sua pia misericordia custodivit" (*Erphurdianus Antiquitatum Variloquus, Incerti Auctoris, nebst einem Anhange historischer Notizen über den Bauernkrieg in und um Erfurt i. J. 1525*, ed. R. Thiele, in *Geschichtsquellen der Provinz Sachsen und angrenzender Gebiete* 42 [Halle, 1906], 133).

4. See Philip N. Bebb, "Jewish Policy in Sixteenth Century Nürnberg," in *Occasional Papers of the American Society for Reformation Research* 1 (1977): 125–36; esp. 132f. Cf. Helmut Veitshans, *Die Judensiedlungen der schwäbischen Reichsstädte und der württembergischen Landstädte im Mittelalter*, Arbeiten zum historischen Atlas von Südwestdeutschland 5 (Stuttgart, 1970), 12–43; 38.

5. See Ludwig Reyscher, *Vollständig historische und kritisch bearbeitete Sammlung der württembergischen Gesetze* (Tübingen, 1831), 4: 60–65.

6. "Quocirca officii nostri esse visum est tante hominum seu potius canum perversitati quocumquemodo resistere . . . " (George, Duke of Bavaria [1486–1529] and Bishop of Speyer [1515–29], *Mandat gegen die Juden* [Hagenau, 4 April 1519; Heinrich Gran], university library, Tübingen; call no.: Gb 599.2⁰).

7. See the literature cited in the introduction by Ernst-Wilhelm Kohls to the edition of Martin Bucer's "A Proposal Concerning Whether It Be Fitting That the Christian Authority Tolerate That the Jews Live Among the Christians, And What Should Be Tolerated, In What Form, and To What Degree" ("Ratschlag, ob christlicher Oberkait gebüren müge, das sye die Juden undter den Christen zu wonen gedulden, und wa sye zu gedulden, wölcher gstalt und mass," [1538/39], in *Martin Bucers Deutsche Schriften*, ed. R. Stupperich [Gütersloh, 1964], 7: 321 n. 3). Special attention should be paid to the article by Wilhelm Maurer, "Martin Butzer und die Judenfrage in Hessen," in *Zeitschrift des Vereins für hessische Geschichte und Landeskunde* 64 (1953): 29–43, and his general, historical overview: *Kirche und Synagoge. Motive und Formen der Auseinandersetzung der Kirche mit dem Judentum im Laufe der Geschichte* (Stuttgart, 1953). Cf. Carl August Hugo Burkhardt, "Die Judenverfolgung im Kurfürstentum Sachsen," *Theologische Studien und Kritiken* 70 (1897): 593–98; 597.

8. For the outbreak of the Judaizing "contagion" in the 1530s, see the letter of King Sigismund of Poland to the Lithuanian senate on 10 July 1539: "We here take the opportunity to inform you that certain persons of Christian faith in this kingdom of ours, the Kingdom of Poland, have converted to the Jewish faith and allowed themselves to be circumcised in the city of Krakow and in sundry other cities of the Kingdom" (E. Zivier, "Jüdische Bekehrungsversuche im 16. Jahrhundert," in *Beiträge zur Geschichte der deutschen Juden, Festschrift Martin Philippsons* [Leipzig, 1916], 86–113; 102). Cf. n. 87 below.

9. On Hieronymus Höltzel, see further in Alfred Gotze, *Die hochdeutschen Drucker der Reformationszeit* (Strasbourg, 1905; reprint ed., Berlin, 1963), 35; Josef Benzing, *Die Buchdrucker des 16. und 17. Jahrhunderts im Deutschen Sprachgebiet* (Wiesbaden, 1963), 331. Most exhaustive of all is Karl Schottenloher, "Die Entwickelung der Buchdruckerkunst in

Franken bis 1530," *Neujahrsblätter,* published by the Gesellschaft für Fränkische Geschichte 5 (Würzburg, 1910), 18–32.

10. Mariä Lichtmess, or "Feast of the Purification of Mary," popular reference to the Feast of the Presentation of our Lord (2 February).

11. The concept "wicked Christian" stems from the language of law. A wicked Christian is anyone who violates the Christian religion on a criminal impulse. Wicked Christians were punished with death by fire. See further in *Sachsenspiegel* Lib. II, 13 §7.

12. Bernau, about twelve and one-half miles northeast of Berlin, was founded at the beginning of the thirteenth century by the Margrave of Bradenburg.

13. That is, the town Knoblauch/Osthavelland, about twenty-two miles west of Berlin, not far from Eltzin.

14. Originally a chalice for the Eucharist, used for the safekeeping of the consecrated host; here, however, the reference is to the tabernacle, or the sacramental pyx, a lidded case by the altar for safeguarding the holy sacrament.

15. A liturgical container for the display and adoration of the consecrated host in prayer and procession.

16. Staaken, not far from Spandau; the distance between Staaken and Knoblauch is about twelve and one-half miles.

17. That is, probably the vicinity of the Spreewald.

18. Stendal, in the district of Magdeburg, the most prosperous city of the Mark Brandenburg until 1488.

19. Matzo, the Jewish pesach bread, made from wheat flour and water, without leavening.

20. Osterburg/Altmark in the district of Magdeburg, city charter, 1296.

21. Born on 21 February 1484; died on 2 July 1535.

22. Celebration of the Feast of the Dispersal of the Apostles.

23. The "Gray Monastery of Berlin," a Franciscan monastery, first mentioned in 1250, and dissolved in 1540. Some of the buildings served from 1574 as a school that later became famous under the name "Gymnasium of the Grey Monastery." Cf. *Germania Sacra,* vol. 1.1: *Das Bistum Brandenburg,* Teil 1 (Berlin, 1929), 371–78 (with bibliography).

24. In what is probably the most important and influential introduction to Luther's writings on the Jews, Ferdinand Cohrs speaks of the "two occasions" in the tract *On the Last Words of David* (1543) on which Luther "approaches anti-Jewishness" (*WA* 54: 16–24; 23f.). Selma Stern-Taeubler actually speaks of Luther's oscillation between love and hatred, in "Die Vorstellung vom Juden und vom Judentum in der Ideologie der Reformationszeit," in *Essays Presented to Leo Baeck on the Occasion of his Eightieth Birthday* (New York: East & West Lib., 1954), 194–211; 202. A more extensive bibliography cannot be given here; see, however, the comprehensive work and bibliography of Johannes Brosseder: *Luthers Stellung zu den Juden im Spiegel seiner Interpreten. Interpretation und Rezeption von Luthers Schriften und Äusserungen zum Judentum im 19. und 20. Jahrhundert vor allem im deutschsprachigen Raum* (München, 1972). C. Bernd Sucher was unable to produce any substantially new insights with his potentially fruitful, Germanistic perspective: *Luthers Stellung zu den Juden.*

Eine Interpretation aus germanistischer Sicht (Nieuwkoop, 1977). The more recent bibliographies overlook an important essay: Joachim Rogge, "Luthers Stellung zu den Juden," *Luther* 40 (1969): 13–24.

25. *Wider die sabbather an einen guten Freund* (1538), WA 50: 312–37; *Von den Juden und ihren Lügen* (1543), WA 53: 417–552; *Vom Schem Hamphoras und vom Geschlecht Christi* (1543), WA 53: 579–648; *Von den letzten Wurten Davids* (1543), WA 54: 28–100.

26. Thus Alfred Falb, *Luther und die Juden. Deutschlands führende Männer und das Judentum,* vol. 4 (München, 1921). Falb sharply marks off a first period of "sympathy toward the Jews" (before and during 1523) from the remaining period of "opposition to the Jews" (ibid., 11–28; 29–73). The same premise is behind the ejaculation of Martin Sasse: "In this hour we hear the voice of the German prophet of the sixteenth century, who out of ignorance began his career as a friend of the Jews, and who, driven by his conscience, his experience and by reality, became the greatest anti-Semite of his age, and warned his nation against the Jews" (*Martin Luther über die Juden: Weg mit ihnen!* ed. M. Sasse [Freiburg, 1938], 2). Even in the more recent literature, there are examples of an isolation of the thematic late writings as a basis for an overall assessment. So Peter Maser, "Luthers Schriftauslegung im Traktat. 'Von den Juden und ihren Lügen' (1543). Ein Beitrag zum 'christologischen Antisemitismus' des Reformators," *Judaica* 29 (1973): 71–84, 149–67. Cf. Otto Clemen in his introduction to Letter no. 3157, *WABr* 8: 89.

27. Paul J. Reiter observes in the Luther of 1540 "a feeling of senility," "depressive, pessimistic bitterness," the revival of "demonomania," and a "preference for expressions that are a little [!] off-color." In the late writings on the Jews he encounters "an indulgence in vulgar and dirty expressions that is striking even when compared with what one is used to hearing from him" (*Martin Luthers Umwelt, Charakter und Psychose sowie die Bedeutung dieser Faktoren für seine Entwicklung und Lehre. Eine historisch-psychiatrische Studie,* vol. 2: *Luthers Persönlichkeit, Seelenleben und Krankheiten* [Kopenhagen, 1941], 205–20; 210).

28. This solution has been offered to explain Luther's later doctrine on the Eucharist. See my counterarguments in *Werden und Wertung der Reformation. Vom Wegestreit zum Glaubenskampf,* 2d ed. (Tübingen, 1979), 368f.=*Masters of the Reformation: Rival Roads to a New Ideology,* trans. Dennis Martin (New York: Cambridge University Press, 1981), 288f.

29. C. B. Sucher makes the lines of demarcation if not explicit then even programmatic: *Luthers Stellung zu den Juden* (cf. n. 24 above). His individual critical remarks indicate that he is especially anxious to distance himself from Wilhelm Maurer, whose outline of church history *in theologicis* gives as reliable an introduction as Reinhold Lewin offers in his presentation of the Luther material: Maurer, *Kirche und Synagoge* (cf. n. 7 above); Lewin, *Luthers Stellung zu den Juden. Ein Beitrag zur Geschichte der Juden in Deutschland während des Reformationszeitalters, Neue Studien zur Geschichte der Theologie und der Kirch* 10 (Berlin, 1911; reprint ed., Aalen, 1973).

30. "I believe that no one can be blessed who is not found in this congregation, acting in accord with it, in one faith, Word, sacrament, hope

and love; and no Jew, heretic, heathen, or sinner will become blessed here, even if he should reconcile with, join, and conform to it in all matters" (*Ein kurcz form der zcehen gepott. D. M. L. Eyn kurcz form des glaubens. Ein kurcz form dess Vatter vnszers, WA* 7: 219, 6–10).

31. In the confession with which Luther concluded his great work on the Eucharist (1528), the Jews are not expressly named: "For the papacy is most certainly that true regiment and tyranny of the Antichrist which sits in the temple of God and rules with human laws, as Christ in Matth. 24 [, 24] and as Paul in 2 Thessalonians 2 [, 4] proclaim. And just as the Turks and all forms of heresy belong in such places of horror as they occupy, so too it is prophesied that the holy seat shall be occupied, but not with the likes of the papacy" (*WA* 26: 506, 40—507, 6). The reason for the *omissio* lies very likely in the emphasis upon the papacy in this passage: in the late medieval accounts of the Antichrist, the Jews are the very first to attach themselves to the Antichrist as "his nation." See Christoph Peter Burger, "Endzeiterwartung im späten Mittelalter," in *Der Antichrist und Die Fünfzehn Zeichen vor dem Jüngsten Gericht* (Hamburg, 1979), 18–53; 39, 43. The earliest connection between Turks and Antichrist is found in the *Dictata* (*WA* 55: II 1. 129, 22–25 [scholion to Ps. 17:3]).

32. "In this way do these articles of faith divide and separate us Christians from all other peoples on earth. For whatever stands outside of Christianity, be it heathens, Turks, Jews, or pseudo-Christians and hypocrites, whether they believe and worship one true God or not, they at least know how God is disposed against them, and not one of them can expect from Him either love or goodness; and so they remain eternally damned by His eternal wrath, for they do not have the LORD Jesus Christ, and so lack the gifts of illumination and grace which only the Holy Ghost can bestow" (*WA* 30: I. 192, 9–16).

33. *WA* 49: 580, 26–37 (sermon printed on 29 September 1544). Cf. "Do you think that if the Turk, pope, Jew, and the whole wicked caboodle, including the Devil, refuse His grace, and instead rage violently against Him, they will elude His strength? They will assuredly find out" (*WA* 54: 37, 33–36; 1543). It is precisely in the context of the confession of faith from the year 1537 (published 1538), that Luther announces for the first time his plan "to thrust our faith up against the madness of the Jews; to see whether some of them might not be won over" (*WA* 50: 280, 9f.).

34. Cf. *WA* 4: 345, 11–19 (scholion to Ps. 118:79; 1514/15).

35. See Scott H. Hendrix, *Ecclesia in Via: Ecclesiological Developments in the Medieval Psalms Exegesis and the Dictata super psalterium (1513–1515) of Martin Luther* (Leiden, 1974), 249–56.

36. "Iudei enim semper sibi impunitatem presumebant, ut patet in multis prophetis, ubi dixerunt 'pax pax,' et non est pax: 'Non veniet super nos malum.' Sicut autem hoc de Iudeis dicitur, ita de Hereticis etc. Quia, ut sepius supra dictum est: [Canon] Quicquid de Iudeis dicitur ad literam, hoc allegorice percutit Iudeos et omnes superbos Christianos, tropologice autem carnales motus et vitia et peccata" (*WA* 3: 177, 25–30 [scholion to Ps. 31:10; ca. 1513]).

37. Augustine, *Enarrationes in Psalmos,* Ps. 52:4; *Corpus Christianorum* 39: 640, 4–13.

38. See Bernhard Blumenkranz, *Les Auteurs chrétiens latins du moyen*

âge sur les juifs et le judaisme (Paris, 1963), 216. Cf. WA 55: I 1. 60, 37—61, 4; note to Ps. 8:3; cf. also Ulrich Mauser, *Der junge Luther und die Häresie* (Gütersloh, 1968), 33–49; 46.

39. "Et quidem Iudei tempore Christi et Apostolorum hoc primo facerunt. Deinde Heretici. Tertio nos miseri pessimi Christiani" (WA 3: 564, 31f. [scholion to Ps. 77]).

40. Cf. WA 3: 563, 31—564, 46.

41. Augustine, *Enarrationes in Psalmos*, Ps. 9:27; *Corpus Christianorum* 38: 70, 5–11. Cf. WA 55: I 1. 67, 22–29; note to Ps. 9:4.

42. *S. Bernardi Opera* (Rome, 1957ff.), 1: 244, 6–25. See my essay "The Shape of Late Medieval Thought: The Birthpangs of the Modern Era," *Archiv für Reformationsgeschichte* 64 (1973): 13–33; 24f. n. 20.

43. For a closer analysis of the *Dictata*, with detailed documentation, see my essay "Die Juden: Ahnen und Geahndete," in *Leben und Werk Martin Luthers von 1526 bis 1546. Festgabe zu seinem 500. Geburtstag, in Auftrag des Theologischen Arbeitkreises für Reformationsgeschichtliche Forschung*, ed. H. Junghans (Berlin, 1983).

44. WA 3: 181, 16 (scholion to Ps. 32:1).

45. WA 3: 203, 4–6; 13–15.

46. WA 55: II 1. 3, 2–10 (scholion to Ps. 1:1).

47. WA 4: 7, 28–30 (scholion to Ps. 84:5). The continuation is found in the scholion to Rom. 10:14: "The Jews, heretics, and schismatics cannot call upon the Lord as long as they are not emancipated by the efficacious proclamation of the Gospel" (WA 56: 422, 7–9).

48. WA 56: 436, 7–20; 16f. (scholion to Rom. 11:22). Cf. Luther's opinion on the Reuchlin affair, dating from 5 August 1514 (WABr 1: no. 9).

49. On this topic, see esp. Joseph Vercruysse, *Fidelis Populus* (Wiesbaden, 1968), 39–51.

50. WA 55: II 1. 69, 8–11 (scholion to Ps. 4:3); WA 3: 501, 31f. (scholion to Ps. 73:9); WA 4: 315, 20–25 (scholion to Ps. 118:20).

51. As Bernhard Blumenkranz has shown, this motif of the "Jews' service" as witness is a special topic in Augustine which was suppressed in the Middle Ages (*Die Judenpredigt Augustins. Ein Beitrag zur Geschichte der jüdisch-christlichen Beziehungen in den ersten Jahrhunderten* [Basel, 1946], 175–81). The overall picture of Augustine is, however, too charitably drawn.

52. WA 3: 568, 10f. (scholion to Ps. 77:9).

53. WA 5: 363, 13–16 (Ps. 11:6).

54. WA 10: I 1. 481, 11; *Kirchenpostille*, 1522.

55. "... plus quam Babylonica captivitas" (WA 2: 215, 2 [1519]); "ut Babylone ipsa confusior sit hodierna ecclesia" (ibid., 226, 22). Cf. *Archiv zur Weimarer Lutherausgabe* (=AWA) (Cologne, 1981), 2: 600, 6–18 (Ps. 9b:9); WA 5: 343, 4–17. From Lyra, Luther was familiar with the interpretation of Psalm 73 in light of the "captivitas babylonica." The uncovering of the *syncera scripturae intelligentia* in *De Captivitate Babylonica* (1520) functions here as a remedy to scriptural misinterpretation; WA 3: 492, 17; cf. ibid., 6: 572, 35f.

56. "Nemo, donec ipse dominus convertat captivitatem plebis suae . . ." (WA 5: 428, 21–25).

57. Ibid., 2: 429, 9–12 (Ps. 13/14:7).

58. Ibid., 5: 429, 1.

59. Ibid., 56: 274, 14 (scholion to Rom. 4:7).

60. In his lecture on the Epistle to the Romans, held in Latin, Luther identifies the theologians of his day who ignore the Scriptures with the German expression, *Sautheologen*—lit. "filthy sow-theologians" (ibid:, 56: 274, 14; 1516).

61. Weimar Luther edition, *Deutsche Bibel* 7: 17, 20–29 (1546).

62. *WA* 57: 87, 21–24 (gloss on Rom. 9: 28f.). Cf. ibid., 56: 95, 25f.

63. *AWA* 2: 230, 27—231, 2 (Ps. 5:4f.); *WA* 5: 131, 23–29.

64. *AWA* 2: 103, 3–7 (Ps. 2:9); *WA* 5: 66, 38—67, 4. Cf. ibid., 7: 486, 6–16 (1521).

65. This is—since R. Lewin, *Luthers Stellung zu den Juden* (cf. n. 29 above), 15 ff.—the accepted explanation. I do not wish to question the fact of such an encounter. The interest of the Jews in Luther is well attested. Haim Hillel Ben-Sasson has documented the hopes for the end of "misery" which in the Jewish community were bound up with the appearance of Luther on the scene. See his outstanding study: "The Reformation in Contemporary Jewish Eyes," in *Proceedings of the Israel Academy of Sciences and Humanities* (Jerusalem, 1971), 4: 239–326; 264–71.

66. *WA* 7: 600, 34. In 1523 this idea becomes thematic in the treatise *Jesus Christ Was Born a Jew*. In a sermon dating from 25 September 1538, the charge is repeated; but it is now clearly directed at the Jews as well: "When we have baptized a Jew, we believe that we have gotten all of him. Afterwards, he is instructed to go to Rome and atone for his sins. But he hasn't been made to understand correctly the Lord's Prayer or our catechism. So now the Jew has abandoned the Laws of Moses, comes to us, and doesn't even receive the Gospel. There he has a nag, here a hack. For he hasn't found the true teaching about Christian faith, and he hasn't had the benefit of guidance from sermons. In the same way did the Jews draw the Gentiles away from their idolatry, but only to lead their following to another idolatry, one which they contrived using their human commandments, and which they should jettison, as we shall shortly hear below" (*WA* 47: 470, 40—471, 7).

67. *AWA* 2: 62, 13—63, 2 (Ps. 1:6); *WA* 5: 46, 20–23.

68. *AWA* 2: 96, 17—97, 3 (Ps. 2:9); *WA* 5: 63, 17–20.

69. With this, I hope to respond to the thesis put foward by James S. Preus, according to which Luther "arbitrarily" rejected in 1522 what he himself introduced in 1523: "The reality at Wittenberg was that the law became incarnated in Luther, himself functioning freely" (*Carlstadt's Ordinaciones and Luther's Liberty: A Study in the Wittenberg Movement 1521–22* [Cambridge: Harvard University Press, 1974], 80).

70. *WA* 51: 196, 16f.; cf. ibid., 53: 530, 25–28; 31f.

71. Ibid., 45: 615, 1–5; cited in Johannes Heckel, *Lex Charitatis. Eine juristische Untersuchung über das Recht in der Theologie Martin Luthers*, ed. Martin Heckel, 2d ed. (Cologne, 1973), 146 n. 765c.

72. "Ego succedo nunc in haereditate nominis, ut senior sim fere Lutherus in mea familia" (*WABr* 5: 351, 29f.; 5 June 1530). Still before opening the letter which contained the news of the death—"It's a shame the messenger couldn't have waited just a minute"—he writes to "Katherin Lutherin" that the glasses which had been sent him were poorly made: "I

couldn't make out a single letter with them" (ibid., 348, 15f). Cf. already on 12 May: "It [my head] refuses to function; I can see very well that age is on its way" (ibid., 316, 16f.).

73. *WABr* 5: 351, 30f. One year later his mother "Hanna" dies; see his last letter of consolation, *WABr* 6: no. 1820 (20 May 1531).

74. In 1521 Luther gives the *Adventspostille* a "trial run," in order to determine the chances for the "de-Babylonization" of the church and to gauge "how the Christians will receive the Gospel after so long and hard a Babylonian captivity" (*WA* 7: 537, 13f.).

75. Ibid., 40: I. 131, 3f.; 1531. Printed 1535; ibid., 21–24; ibid., 40: II. 92, 5f. Cf. *WAT* 2, no. 2241 and no. 2255 (1531); no. 1820 and 2797 (1532).

76. *WA* 38: 195, 17–22; 1533. See my "Dichtung und Wahrheit. Das Wesen der Reformation aus der Sicht der Confutatio," in *Confessio Augustana und Confutatio. Der Augsburger Reichstag 1530 und die Einheit der Kirche*, ed. E. Iserloh (Münster, 1980), 217–31; 228f.

77. This last hesitation of Luther—whose worries began to grow, from the end of 1518 (*WABr* 1: 282, 17–22)—is in my estimation attested in a letter to Spalatin on 24 February 1520, written under the impact of Laurentius Valla's work on the Donation of Constantine (with a dedication from Hutten, 1520) which he had just read (ibid., 2: 48, 26f.). While Luther grounded his Antichrist interpretation of the pope in the Bible (see ibid., 1: 270, 12f.; 2 Thess. 2:4), he here points to the Antichrist, "quem vulgata opinione," the world is expecting. For a reliable analysis of the development of Luther's image of the papacy, see Scott H. Hendrix, *Luther and the Papacy: Stages in a Reformation Conflict* (Philadelphia: Fortress Press, 1981).

78. *WA* 54: 206–99 (1545).

79. Ibid., 54: 361–73 (1545), 363, and appendix, illustration 9. Cf. also Luther's parodies of the Benedicite, the Gratias, Paternoster, and Ave Maria directed against the pope (ibid., *WA* 60: 177–79 [1546]).

80. Ibid., 30: II. 116f. (1528); cited by Helmut Lamparter, *Luthers Stellung zum Türkenkrieg* (München, 1940), 20. Just as in the early phase of the Reformation Luther is prepared to offer a "qualified" defense of the Jews; in a written opinion on the Turks to Spalatin, dating from 15 December 1518, we hear: "I think I can show that Rome today is worse than the Turks" (*WABr* 1. 270, 13f.). This assessment of the Turks is on the whole the counterpart to the 1523 treatise on the Jews. See further Harvey Buchanan, "Luther and the Turks 1519–1529," *Archiv für Reformationsgeschichte* 47 (1956): 145–60. For the interpretation of the Turks as the "instrument of God" in the apocalyptic visions of the sixteenth century, see Klaus Deppermann, *Melchior Hoffman. Soziale Unruhen und apokalyptische Visionen im Zeitalter der Reformation* (Göttingen, 1979), 183, 186.

81. For the connection between "Gog" and the Antichrist, we have the testimony of the baptized Jew Johannes Gratia Dei: "It is absolutely clear that this 'Gog' is what the Christians call the 'Antichrist'—the majority of you Jews follow hard on his heels in the belief that he is the Messiah whom you are vainly awaiting"—". . . non dubitatur quin ipse [Gog] sit, quem Christiani 'Antichristum' appellant, qui a maiori parte vestrum [you unconverted Jews] sequetur putantes ipsum esse Messiam, quem frustra expectatis" (*Liber de confutatione hebrayce secte* [Rome, 1500], fol. 78ᵛ). The

Jews' connection with the Turks is made through the supposed return, at the end of time, of the Jews to Jerusalem through Turkey. The "red Jews," five hundred thousand to six hundred thousand in number, are supposed to have arrived in 1523 at Egypt from Africa, only a thirty days' journey from Jerusalem. This is the report which is reprinted by Otto Clemen in *Flugschriften aus den ersten Jahren der Reformation* (Halle, 1906/7; reprint ed., Nieuwkopp, 1967), 1: 442–44.

82. See Luther's earlier letters to Wenzeslaus Link (7 March 1529) and to Nikolaus Hausmann (26 October 1528); *WABr* 5: 28, 22f.; 166, 13f.

83. *WA* 30: II. 225, 17 (1530). Cf. *WADB* 7: 416, 306. In April 1529, in his great work *On the Wars Against the Turks*, Luther concluded, ". . . as the pope is the Antichrist, so is the Turk the Devil incarnate. . . . In sum, as it is written, where the spirit of lies rules, there the spirit of death can be found too . . ." (*WA* 30: II. 126, 1–7). The correlation between Turks and Antichrist is already made in Luther's interpretation of Psalm 1 (ibid., 3: 505, 26), again in a context of Jews and teachers of falsehoods. Cf. Luther's classification of Jews, Turks, and Papists in his table talk in 1532–33 (*WAT* 3, no. 2863).

84. *WABr* 5: 285, 7–10; 24 April 1530.

85. *WAT* 1: 135, 15f. (no. 330); cited by Ulrich Asendorf, *Eschatologie bei Luther* (Göttingen), 205.

86. *Von der Wiedertaufe an zwei Pfarrherrn* (early 1528); *WA* 26: 170, 30—171, 2. The capacity for salvation inherent in the sacrament of the new dispensation, and lacking in the old, is a firmly established theme of scholastic theology which, at first employed against Luther, was likewise brought to bear in anti-Jewish polemics. See the highly interesting "dogmatics" of the converted Jew, Hadrianus Finus: *In Iudaeos flagellum ex sacris scriptis excerptum*, written ca. 1520 in Ferrara, but first published in 1538 by his son Daniel; esp. pars. IV, cap. 8, concl. 4–10, fol. 117ᵛ–120ʳ.

87. *WA* 50: 309. See also Erasmus's reports from the years 1533 and 1535: "Nunc audimus apud Bohemos exoriri novum Judaeorum genus, Sabbatarios appelant. . ." (*De amabili* [Allen: *Liber de sarcienda*] *Ecclesiae concordia*, with dedication to Julius Pflug dating from 31 July 1533. Erasmus, *Opera omnia* [Leiden, 1704], 5: cols. 505D–506A). Cf. "Dicuntur et hodie repullulascere Sabbatarii, qui septimi diei otium incredibili superstitione observant" (*Ecclesiastae, sive de ratione concionandi* Lib. III, with dedication to Christoph von Stadion dating from 6 August 1535, ibid., col. 1038B). George H. Williams placed the "Sabbatarii" in the context of a comprehensive "Judaizing" movement which in the late fifteenth century seized all of Christianity," with important centers in Novgorod between 1470 and 1516, and in Lithuania from ca. 1530 ("Protestants in the Ukraine During the Period of the Polish-Lithuanian Commonwealth," *Harvard Ukrainian Studies* 2 [1978]: 41–72; 46). Williams characterizes the Sabbatarians as the extreme wing of this pan-European movement, and in particular, as those "who were virtually converts to Judaism" (ibid., 47). King Sigismund possibly sought less to ward off "unorthodox" influences from Germany (Prussia) than from the Ukraine and Lithuania. Cf. n. 8 above; for Luther, cf. also n. 66 above.

88. Cf. E. Zivier, *Jüdische Bekehrungsversuche im 16. Jahrhundert* (cf. n. 8 above), 96–113. Although we can now state with considerable confidence

that the Sabbatarians of the 1530s comprised a Judaizing wave of major significance, the "scapegoat" theory of Jerome Friedman is not thereby refuted. The reactions to the Sabbatarians were not groundless, and they were certainly not the work of Luther's central controlling influence: "That Jewry was chosen as the scapegoat to account for that form of Protestant irregularity known as Sabbatarianism was symptomatic of a form of anti-Semitism endemic in the Christianity of that age which continued to see the Jew as a very powerful agent of destruction and corruption. That Luther was so central to creating these attitudes in Germany is just one more indication of his central importance" (Jerome Friedman, "Sebastian Münster, the Jewish Mission, and Protestant Antisemitism," *Archiv für Reformationsgeschichte* 70 [1979]: 238–59, 258; idem, "The Reformation and Jewish Antichristian Polemics," *Bibliothèque d'Humanisme et Renaissance* 41 [1979]: 83–97).

89. WA 50: 313, 12–15.

90. WAT 1: 427, 6–10; 8 (no. 864).

91. Ibid., 1: 427, 9f.

92. Heinrich Bornkamm supplies a handy and precise encapsulation of the "modern innovation" in the writings on the Turks: "In place of the crusades Luther substitutes the eschatological war. This exchange marks a deep-seated change in motives" (*Martin Luther in der Mitte seines Lebens. Das Jahrzehnt zwischen dem Wormser und dem Augsburger Reichstag*, ed. K. Bornkamm [Göttingen, 1979], 515–26; 525).

93. WABr 5: 166, 13f.; to Nikolau Hausmann, 26 October 1529.

94. Ibid., 5: 175, 12f.; to Jakob Propst, 10 November 1529.

95. "Germania plena est proditoribus, qui Turcae favent" (ibid., 5: 175, 7f.).

96. Johannes Pfefferkorn, *Speculum adhortationis Judaice ad Christum* (Cologne, 1507), fol. C 4ᵛ–D 1ʳ. It is likely that after 1497 more exiled Iberian Jews found refuge in Turkey than in all other countries combined. See Wlad. W. Kaplun-Kogan, *Die Wanderbewegungen der Juden* (Bonn, 1913), 43. The Jews, moreover, soon took control of Turkish trade (ibid., 156 n. 56).

97. See C. A. H. Burkhardt, "Die Judenverfolgungen . . . " (cf. n. 7 above), 596–98.

98. WABr 8: 77–78; Wolfgang Capito to Luther, 26 April 1537. See Selma Stern, *Josel von Rosheim. Befehlshaber der Judenschaft im Heiligen Römischen Reich Deutscher Nation* (Stuttgart, 1959), 126. Cf. Raphael Loewe, "Christian Hebraists (1100–1890)," in *Encyclopedia Judaica* (Jerusalem, 1971), 8: 10–72. See above all, Jerome Friedman, "Sixteenth-Century Christian-Hebraica: Scripture and the Renaissance Myth of the Past," *Sixteenth Century Journal* 11.4 (1980): 67–85.

99. See Part One, 68 n. 41 above.

100. WABr 8: 90, 1; 46–50; 32f.; 91, 56–60; to Josel of Rosheim, 11 June 1537.

101. WA 51: 195, 29–32.

102. Ibid., 195, 39f.

103. Ibid., 196, 4–17.

104. Ibid., 196, 5.

105. Cf. the extensive comment in ibid., 53: 527, 15–31.

106. Cf. the "incredible story," 97–99 above and the appendix, 147–49 below.

107. Cf. *WA* 53: 482, 12–14 n. 6. Though the *WA* editor alludes in passing to Eck, a thorough comparison leads one to suspect that Luther had this work against Osiander—whom Eck chides as "Luther-son" and "Jew-father"—on his desk before him.

108. Graft and the purchase of privileges are always possibilities, by which means—as Luther on 9 February 1544 complains—the Jews in the Mark Brandenburg and in Prague "rule" with their money (*WABr* 10: 526, 8–13). Cf. Luther's charge, which Agricola lamented in his autobiography: "Me insimulavit, quod et munus acceperim a Judaeis. Et quod depravatis scripturis defenderem Judaeos" (E. Theile, "Denkwürdigkeiten aus dem Leben des Johann Agricola von Eisleben. Von ihm selbst aufgezeichnet," *Theologische Studien und Kritiken* 80 [1907]: 246–270; 270 and n. 2).

109. *WA* 53: 526, 7–16; 528, 31–34. Cf. 520, 33—521, 7. In the same year (1543) two other writings on the Jews saw print: *Vom Schem Hamphoras* (ibid., 53: 579–648) and the relatively temperate *On the Last Words of David* (ibid., 54: 28–100), in which Luther lays out his arguments against the rabbinical exegesis of the Scriptures in order to prove that the Messianic prophecy is a prefiguration of Christ.

110. Ibid., 53: 449, 26–29. As has been said, the Anabaptists were prefectly capable of representing the *"haeretici"* in this chain: "Non de ocio cogitandum est, nobis praesertim, qui in Ecclesia docemus. Pugnandum est nobis undique cum diaboli agminibus. Hac nostra aetate quam varios hostes vidimus? Defensores idolorum Papae, Iudaeos, monstra Anabaptistarum multiplicia, Servetos et alios" (preface to Bibliander's Koran edition, ibid., 572, 9–12).

111. This is the religion of performance, that "rational" principle of *do ut des* which, bypassing the person and works of Christ seeks to obtain the grace of God for itself through rites, laws, and works: "That is the religio Papae, Iudaeorum, Turcarum . . . 'si sic fecero, erit mihi deus clemens'" (ibid., 40: I. 603, 6–10; on Gal. 4:8, cf. ibid., 10: I. 465, 4f. [1522]; on the dual-nature-of-man doctrine: ibid., 20: 345, 19–37; ibid., 54: 37, 29–38 [1543]; summary: ibid., 49: 580, 26–37 [sermon from 29 September 1544]).

112. For the widespread importance of the conception of the Antichrist during the Middle Ages, see Marjorie Reeves, *The Influence of Prophecy in the Later Middle Ages: A Study in Joachimism* (Oxford: At the Clarendon Press, 1969), esp. 358–74; and idem, "Some Popular Prophecies from the Fourteenth to the Seventeenth Centuries," in *Studies in Church History*, vol. 8: *Popular Belief and Practice*, ed. G. J. Cuming and D. Baker (Cambridge: Cambridge University Press, 1972), 107–34, esp. 122f. Bernard McGinn, *Visions of the End: Apocalyptic Traditions in the Middle Ages* (New York: Columbia University Press, 1979). For the general currency of the Antichrist theme in Luther's time, see Gustav Adolf Benrath, *Das Verständnis der Kirchengeschichte in der Reformationszeit* (in press).

113. "Hoc anno (1540) numerus annorum Mundi precise est. 5500. Quare sperandus est finis mundi. Nam sextus Millenarius non complebitur. Sicuti tres dies mortui Christi non sunt completi . . . " (*WA* 53: 171, 1–9).

114. Cf. n. 6 above.

115. See Part Two, 75–79 above.

116. See Part One, 47–50 above.

117. An investigation of this tradition in England is already underway: Bryan W. Ball, *A Great Expectation: Eschatological Thought in English Protestantism to 1660* (Leiden: E. J. Brill, 1975), 146–55; Paul Christianson, *Reformers and Babylon: English Apocalyptic Visions from the Reformation to the Eve of the Civil War* (Toronto: University of Toronto Press, 1978), 210–12; Mel Scult, *Millennial Expectations and Jewish Liberties: A Study of the Efforts to Convert the Jews in Britain, up to the Mid-Nineteenth Century* (Leiden: E. J. Brill, 1978), 15–34.

118. Jacob Revius, *Over-ysselsche sangen en dichten,* ed. W.A.P. Smit (Amsterdam, 1930), 222; cf. *Protestantse poëzie der 16de en 17de eeuw,* ed. K. Heeroma (Amsterdam, 1940), 179; L. Strengholt, *Bloemen in Gethsemané. Verzamelde studies over de dichter Revius* (Amsterdam, 1976), 116–20.

119. As far as I am aware, for the first time in *Ein Sermon von der Betrachtung des heiligen Leidens Christi,* 1519: "And so you will be more filled with anxiety when you reflect on Christ's suffering; for the evil-doers, the Jews, seeing that God has now tried them and driven them into Diaspora, have indeed been the servants of your sins; and you are truly the ones whose sin caused God to snuff out and crucify the life of his son, as is written in the Scriptures" (*WA* 2: 138, 29–32; cf. ibid., 9: 652, 16–24 [1521]; ibid., 28: 233, 1f. [1528]).

120. Ibid., 35: 576. Cf. *WAT* 6: 257, no. 6897.

121. See n. 38 above.

122. In the eighteenth century the "Jew-detector" was implemented entirely in the spirit of Luther by Johann Georg Hamann (d. 1788) in an autobiographical passage: "I recognized my own wrong in the history of the Jewish nation, read therein my own life's course, and thanked God for looking after this nation of his, because nothing apart from such an example could entitle me to an equal hopefulness" (Johann Georg Hamann, *Sämtliche Werke,* ed. J. Nadler, 6 vols. [Vienna, 1949–57], 2: 40, 25–29; cited by Oswald Bayer, "Wer bin ich? Gott als Autor meiner Lebensgeschichte," *Theologische Beiträge* 11 [1980]: 245–61; 254).

123. B. Blumenkranz has assembled an interesting, but by no means exhaustive, collection of citations around the theme of the Jews' "sole responsibility" for the death of Christ: *Les Auteurs chrétiens* (cf. n. 38 above), 86 (no. 92f.: Gregory the Great); 134 (no. 119g: Beda Venerabilis); 262 (no. 226b: Cardinal Humbert). Cf. also the results of his study on the interpretation of the prayer *Pro Iudaeis* in the Maundy Thursday service ("Perfidia," *Archivum Latinitatis Medii Aevi* 22 [1952]: 157–70; reprinted in *Juifs et Chrétiens. Patristique et Moyen Age* [London, 1977], VII). The much-read theologian from Tübingen, Gabriel Beil (d. 1495), needed no authoritative proof to be convinced that Christ's voluntary sacrificial death did not at all relieve the Jews of the onus of sole responsibility: ". . . ut voluntarie seipsum pro nobis offerret, non excusat Iudeos ab homicidio, quod fecerunt maliciose . . . " (Lectio 82D, *Gabrielis Biel. Canonis Misse expositio,* ed. H. A. Oberman and W. J. Courtenay [Wiesbaden, 1967], 4: 50, 29ff.; cf. Lectio 87D–F, 144, 25f.; 146, 8. So, too, similarly Reuchlin in his *Augenspiegel* [Tübingen: Thomas Anshelm, 1511], fol. H 3ᵛ). Luther's

teacher and superior, Johannes von Staupitz, charged the Jews primarily with cruelty in his sermon on the Passion, dating from 1512: "O you evil Jew! Pilate teaches you that your character is harsher than a pig's; the pig at least knows mercy" (*Salzburger Passionspredigten*, 1512, Sermon X, Salzburg, Klosterbibliothek St. Peter, call no. b. V. 8, fol. 39^r, in Johannes von Staupitz, *Sämtliche Schriften*, ed. Graf zu Dohna von Lothar and R. Wetzel, vol. 3: *Deutsche Schriften*, I [Berlin, 1983]). Alluding to Luke 23:25, he charges the Jews with purposely having tortured Christ: "the Jews inflicted the harshest damage on the Lord in all matters and with all torments, and so savagely struck him with hand and foot that the whole of his body was seized with quivering and trembling" (Sermon XI, fol. 47^v; on Luke 23:25, see Sermon X, fol. 41^v–43^r). The Erfurt Augustinian Magister Johannes von Paltz (d. 1511) had already accused the Jews of knowingly and willingly torturing the Lord: " . . . quidquid erat poenalius et confusibilius, Iudaei in poena Christi elegerunt" (Johannes von Paltz OESA, *Opera*, vol. 1: *Coelifodina*, ed. C. P. Burger and F. Stasch [Berlin, 1983], 50, 28).

124. "Hic est locus, ex quo debemus facere canticum und frolich sein, ut non sic recordemur passionis Christi, quomodo zusingen 'der arm Judas,' und stechen den Iudaeis die augen aus. . . . Yhr habt wol euber euch [Christen] zu weinen, quod estis damnatae et peccatrices. Ideo ipse flet et patitur pro nobis" (*WA* 36: 136, 29–32, 36—137, 2 [sermon from 24 March 1532]).

Epilogue:
The Stony Path to Coexistence

Europe's passage to toleration was a slow and arduous process. The timid beginnings in the sixteenth century came at the expense of the Jews, particularly in Germany. What lines of connection run through humanism and the Reformation to the breakthrough of toleration during the Enlightenment? Can one of the three major figures studied above be claimed as the champion and model of this development? Was it Reuchlin, the master of the three classical languages, who came to the defense of civil rights for Jews? Or Erasmus, the incorruptible editor of the New Testament, who pleaded the cause of peace and harmony in the church and in society? Or even Luther, the fearless prophet of a truly secular state freed from church control?

To our age the answer is axiomatic: the unbroken thread of humanitarianism obviously runs from Reuchlin and Erasmus to Hobbes, Voltaire, and Lessing. No one has demonstrated the continuity more eloquently or with more insight than Peter Gay in his magnificent study of the Enlightenment. A single quotation from his work *The Enlightenment: An Interpretation*, with the programmatic subtitle *The Rise of Modern Paganism*, will be sufficient to illustrate his central thesis. Catholicism and Protestantism had wound up in a cul-de-sac in which they were hopelessly entangled and from which they could not by their own efforts extricate themselves. A genuine alternative, Peter Gay tells us, lay open to Europe: "The humanists had prepared the way for that solution; their realism made possible a secular view of political power and a secular, or at least no longer specifically Christian, justification for political obligation; their critical philology, combined with their admiration for antiquity, prepared educated men to read Christian documents with skeptical detachment, and pagan philosophies with sympathy; their appeal to nature laid the foundations for . . . a style of thought that ordered the world by natural law, natural morality, and natural theology."[1]

The history of the Jews in Europe seems to fit this pattern to a nicety. In the age of confessionalism, particularly in the seventeenth century, the Jews had no grounds to suspect that the Dark Ages were finally a thing of the past. It was not until the Enlightenment perforated the Christian world view that the air of freedom finally wafted their way. Yet here the sources become uncooperative; they refuse to agree on that straight line leading from humanism to Enlightenment—bypassing the Reformation. This lack of unanimity is not to be blamed on Peter Gay, nor does it detract from the farsightedness of his work. It is more a question of a flaw in the foundations on which all Enlightenment scholarship is laid. To begin with, the central figures of the sixteenth century are painted in colors that are too modern and too tolerant. Even the most distinguished driving forces of the humanistic movement, Reuchlin and Erasmus, are in their roles as Enlightenment thinkers overtaxed and overburdened. Reuchlin does indeed plead the case for civil rights, but he never doubts the collective guilt of the Jews or the utility of mass expulsion. Erasmus promotes the cause of tolerance among educated Christians and of freedom in research and teaching, but at the same time rejoices in the fact that France is free of heretics and Jews.

A further and more serious "structural flaw" must be remedied by reconstruction. The Reformation studies of this century were at first centered exclusively on the figure of Luther. With equal exclusivity, the research of the last decades has concentrated on the vital connection between civic freedom and Reformation faith in the cities. But to achieve a total picture, a third phase needs to be included alongside Luther and this civic Reformation: the "Third Reformation," which takes its direction and name from the Geneva reformer John Calvin (d. 1564) and is thus called Calvinism.

In the second decade of the sixteenth century, the cities resonated so strongly with Luther's voice that the evangelical movement was able to survive the critical phase of ecclesiastical excommunication and imperial outlawry. Beset for decades by social tensions, and well versed in church criticism from the lowest to the highest echelons, the cities could easily change from mere loading platforms for news and ideas into integrated relay stations of the Reformation that pulsed with political action and agitation, with sermons and printed matter. The significance of the Reformation for the cities is thus far uncontested. But civic Reformation was just an episode, a brief burst of activity that lasted no longer than a decade, reaching its peak in the late 1520s and subsiding even before midcentury under the irresistible pressure of the emperor.

The "Third Reformation" owes its existence to precisely this political and juridical weakening of the cities. The imperial Interim of 1548 and the religious mandate that followed the military defeat of the evangelical orders sealed the irreversible development that ultimately transformed the imperial city into the district or county town.[2] The bearers of the Third Reformation were refugees—fugitives from the southern German, French, and soon also Netherlandish cities. In the duration and extent of its impact alone, this movement was more successful than its early counterparts. Its interpretation of the gospel of grace and faith was shaped by the contours of its diaspora experience.[3] Justification of the godless was now actually experienced in the deliverance of the homeless. One of the outstanding features of the "Third Reformation" was the new stance taken toward the "miserable" Jews. Exile, and not the castigation of the Jews, became the distinctive mode of existence for God's people in all ages.

The second upsurge of the Reformation, to which Luther's rediscovery of the gospel had lent a peculiar character within the city walls, began under the banner of the common good, civic freedom, and civil rights. This Reformation was united in its longing for a realization of the so patently absent *corpus Christianum*, and for reshaping the city into a model of Christian fellowship founded upon unblemished dogma and conduct, and therefore (!) also "Jew-free." The extent and the boundaries of civic freedom were set by the Christian faith.

Urban reformers like Huldreich Zwingli in Zurich and Martin Bucer in Strasbourg never condoned Luther's outbursts against the Jews, and even faulted him in their embarrassment for his coarse vulgarisms. But they nonetheless shared his basic conviction that the Jews as Jews, that is, the unbaptized Jews, threatened the common good.[4] Christian Hebraists like Andreas Osiander in Nuremberg and Wolfgang Capito in Strasbourg pioneered with foundational, widereaching undertakings in the field of Old Testament interpretation, and they conveyed their deep respect for Judaism or rather for Judaic erudition.[5] Although standing on the shoulders of their teacher Reuchlin, in one respect they remained indebted to the civic Reformation; they never made Reuchlin's defense of the secular rights of Jews into a concerted program. Even Osiander, derided as a "Jewfather" and in actual fact a courageous and outspoken opponent of libelous Jew-baiting, never overcame the limitations of a socially and religiously determined picture of a "Jew-free prosperity."

Once the homeless, fugitive Christians were compelled to share the destiny of the Jews, expulsion no longer bore the unambiguous marks of a God-sent punishment. The destiny of worldwide diaspora, formerly the proof of the obstinate Jew's guilt, was now the badge of faith of the avowed Christian. In the late sermons of Calvin, delivered in French and only recently published in a modern edition,[6] we encounter a growing sense of the hidden community of fate shared by Christians and Jews in their homeless state of persecution and diaspora.[7]

This view of God's covenant as one held in common by Christians and Jews, utterly inconceivable from Augustine to Erasmus and Luther, now spread in two directions—by way of France and the Netherlands to England and Scotland, and eventually to North America.[8] The old and the new dispensations now fused together into the one testament of the undivided Holy Scriptures. Such a consolidation became possible through the discovery of a God who, faithful and steadfast, always keeps his word, without ever being fazed by the disobedience of his people, be they Jews or Christians. From the beginnings of the Reformation, the only reformer even to approximate this future-oriented view was Luther's disciple Justas Jonas.

In the course of the seventeenth century—first in Holland, then in England, and finally in several settlements of the New World as well—Jews were granted, above and beyond protection, also certain civil rights. In 1657, the United Netherlands required that their Jews abroad be recognized as citizens of the state,[9] an act of emancipation that, in contrast with the short-term improvements in status prompted elsewhere in Europe by enlightened absolutism and the French Revolution,[10] would never again be repealed. Wherever the "Third Reformation" sought to escape its ordained homelessness by seizing political hegemony, it struck the limit of its own liberating powers. But in those places to which the diaspora compelled or confined it, the "Third Reformation" made its deepest impression upon the modern era.[11]

This "Third Reformation" did not have to purchase its impact on modern times by sacrificing its roots in the age of humanism and Reformation. The movement owed its vitality to those unlikely confederates who only now, in virtue of their combined effect, could truly be called a triumvirate. Luther's programmatic Reformation writings from 1520 formed the unmistakable basis of the "Third

Reformation." Explication of the Old Testament was modelled after the Christian Hebraists who considered themselves Reuchlin's pupils. And lastly, the adoption of Erasmian ideas by this third-reformational force in the seventeenth century was possible only because its own roots were deeply implanted in the civic Reformation, which in turn owed to Erasmus of Rotterdam its integration of learning and piety with the ideal of the common weal. In their reinterpretation by the "Third Reformation," Reuchlin, Erasmus, and Luther are divested of their anti-Judaism and can now, together, be of service to the new awakening to solidarity that none of them had foreseen.

With this in mind, we may venture one thesis and one hypothesis.

First the thesis. The first visible advances in the direction of tolerance cannot be traced back to a "new paganism." Neither are they attributable to the vanguard of the Enlightenment, whether the elitist "deists" John Locke (d. 1704) and David Hume (d. 1776) in England or the *philosophes* such as Montesquieu (d. 1755) or Voltaire (d. 1778) in pre-revolutionary France, not to speak of the late Enlightenment in Germany. Certainly a rise of paganism did take place, but to be precise it was the rise of the non-Jews, of the *goyim*, which continued well into the twentieth century, with all its attendant consequences.

And now for the hypothesis. Religious fanaticism, which over the centuries has been hammered equally deeply into the minds of both the elite and the uneducated strata, can be expunged or expelled only through an equally effective antidote. If this does not happen, then beneath the enlightened surface of our modern, pluralistic society the furnace of fear will ignite, as the most recent European history shows. Nothing is as dangerous as the desire to shout down this fear with outcries that declare the Nazi era an "unrepeatable" period of criminality, that present it as an aberration in a world which is in and of itself enlightened, and that disarm it as something "typically German." Unless these images of hatred are dislodged at their roots, we will not be immune to the resurgence of anti-Semitism from out of the glowing ashes of an "unrepeatable" past. Nothing is more dangerous, because nothing is less predictable than the coalition between ancient religious fear and modern unreligious optimism.

The "Third Reformation," too, had its own historical rise and fall. In Europe, beginning with the eighteenth century and then rapidly and appreciably, thereafter, it forfeited its persuasive powers as—anti-intellectual, anticultural, and introverted—it detached itself from the heritage of Reuchlin and his contemporaries, Erasmus and Luther. Today, where in its political and moral participation it still demonstrates a strong and vital will, the "third force" finds itself labeled puritanical, fundamentalist, or biblicist, and is banished into the past. In this way, we run the risk of severing ourselves from those who even now hold fast to the value of conjoining faith and the common weal. This heritage contains something ready-made and indispensable to any attempt at finally uncovering the roots of anti-Semitism: the view of a common persecution and the insistence on a single foundation for the solidarity of Jews and Christians, anchored in God's plan for history. How far the toleration of the Enlightenment can take Jews and Christians is obvious; a sharp increase in Arab oil prices and the misguided bombs of Israel suddenly lay bare the limits. Toleration remains a catchword when it rests on a bad conscience. Coexistence between Christians and Jews only has a future in the presence of a common history finally understood, a history in which both are bound by the covenant with God—despite hatred and collective guilt, despite expulsion, persecution, and annihilation.

Notes to Epilogue

1. Peter Gay, *The Enlightenment: An Interpretation—The Rise of Modern Paganism*, vol. 1 (New York: W. W. Norton, 1977), 297.

2. Cf. Gustave Bossert, *Das Interim in Württemberg* (Halle, 1895), 95–105; Thomas A. Brady, Jr., *Ruling Class, Regime and Reformation at Strasbourg, 1520–1555* (Leiden, 1978), 275ff.; Erdmann Weyrauch, *Konfessionelle Krise und soziale Stabilität. Das Interim in Strassburg (1548–1562)* (Stuttgart, 1978), 159ff.

3. Just as the Huguenots were in a position to feel almost tolerated, they experienced the trauma of the St. Bartholomew's Day massacre on 24 August 1572; this is comparable to the impact of the Interim upon German Protestantism. On this, see Robert M. Kingdon, *Geneva and the Consolidation of the French Protestant Movement, 1564–1572: A Contribution to the History of Congregationalism, Presbyterianism, and Calvinist Resistance Theory* (Geneva, 1967), 200f.

4. See Reinhold Lewin, *Luthers Stellung zu den Juden. Ein Beitrag zur Geschichte der Juden in Deutschland während des Reformationszeitalters* (Berlin, 1911; reprint ed., Aalen, 1973), 98f.; J. Cohrs, *WA* 54: 20f. Cf. also the extensive material provided by John W. Kleiner, "The Attitudes of the Strasbourg Reformers toward Jews and Judaism," Master's thesis, Temple University, Philadelphia, 1978. On Martin Bucer, see Dr. Kroner, "Die Hofpredigerpartei und die Juden unter Philipp von Hessen," in *Das Jüdische Literaturblatt* 11 (1882): 165f.; 169f.; Wilhelm Maurer, "Martin Bucer und die Judenfrage in Hessen," in *Zeitschrift des Vereins für hessische Geschichte und Landeskunde* 65 (1953): 29–43.

5. On Osiander, see Andreas Osiander d. Ä., *Gesamtausgabe,* vol. 3: *Schriften und Briefe 1528 bis April 1530,* ed. G. Müller and G. Seebass (Gütersloh, 1979), 335–40, and corresponding bibliographical references. On Capito, see James M. Kittelson, *Wofgang Capito. From Humanist to Reformer* (Leiden: E. J. Brill, 1975), 21f.; 25f.; 33f.; 211f.

6. Sermon dating from 8 July 1549 (Jer. 16:1–7): "Quant donc nous voyons que nous sommes pareilz aux Juifz, nous avons que nous sommes pareilz aux Juifz, nous avons ung mireoir pour congnoistre rebellion contre Dieu. Or quant il nous chastiera bien rudement, pourrons nous dire qu'il n'a pas assez attendu et que de nostre costé nous ne nous sommes pas monstrez incorrigibles jusques au bout? Ainsi donc, quant nous lisons ce passage, aprenons de ne point condampner les Juifz mais nous mesmes, et de con-

gnoistre que nous ne vallons pas myeulx, et que s'il y a eu alors une telle brutalité que la parolle de Dieu n'ait de rien servy, que aujourdhuy il y en a autant ou plus" (Johannes Calvin, *Sermons sur les Livres de Jérémie et des Lamentations*, ed. R. Peter, Supplementa Calviniana 6 [Neukirchen-Vluyn, 1971], 59, 12–18). Sermon from 10 July 1549 (Jer. 16:12–15): "Et combien que nous ne soyons pas de la race d'Abraham et de ce peuple qui a esté delivré d'Egipte, neantmoins pource que nous representons ce peuple là, ceste delivrance ne nous doibt point sortir des aureilles" (ibid., 78, 27–29). Sermon of 6 September 1550 (Lam. 1:1, introduction): " . . . sy on faict comparaison avec ceux dont parle icy le prophete on trouverra que nous commes beaucoup pires que ceulx là de son temps" (ibid., 183, 34—184, 1).

7. A. J. Visser comes to a different conclusion, based on older material: *Calvijn en de Joden*, supplement to *Kerk en Israel* 17 ('s Gravenhage, 1963), esp. 18. Likewise, Jacques Courvoisier: " . . . what Calvin has to say on this topic is of no great importance" ("Calvin und die Juden. Zu einem Streitgespräch," in *Christen und Juden. Ihr Gegenüber vom Apostelkonzil bis heute*, ed. W. D. Marsch and K. Thieme [Mainz, 1961], 141–46; 146; first published in *Judaica* 2 [1946], 203–8).

8. For an assessment of the situation seen from the Jewish perspective, see Haim Hillel Ben-Sasson, "The Reformation in Contemporary Jewish Eyes," in *Proceedings of the Israel Academy of Sciences and Humanities* 4 (1969–70): 239–329; 286f. In the Jewish perspective, the Third Reformation is only a further sign of the breakdown of the *Corpus Christianum*. As was true in the case of the Hussite movement, this is, naturally, not a negative sign: " . . . the antihierarchical, anti-monastic and iconoclastic tendencies characterizing the Hussite movement [is considered] to be a change in the right direction. . . . The rise of Luther in Germany occurred at the time when Jews were in particular need of encouragement" (ibid., 255).

9. See J. van den Berg, *Joden en Christenen in Nederland gedurende de zeventiende eeuw, Verkenning en Bezinning* 3, no. 2 (Kampen, 1969); cf. "Eschatological Expectations Concerning the Conversion of the Jews in the Netherlands During the Seventeenth Century," in *Puritans, the Millennium and the Future of Israel: Puritan Eschatology, 1600–1660*, ed. P. Toon (Cambridge: James Clarke, 1970), 137–53. See also in this connection Robert M. Healey, "The Jew in Seventeenth-Century Protestant Thought," *Church History* 46 (1977): 63–79; 64. On 13 December 1619, Holland and Westfriesland granted to the cities in their domain the right to enact laws of their own for regulating their relationships to "the Hebrew nation." This document was published by J. Meijer, *Hugo de Groot: Remonstrantie nopende de ordre dije in de landen van Hollandt ende Westvrieslandt dijent gestelt op de Joden* (Amsterdam, 1949), 101. The most important document is the liberalization proposed by Hugo Grotius. Also most revealing is the anonymous Jewish reaction to the proposed legislation expressed about 1617; ibid., Appendix C, 141–43. See also W. J. M. van Eysinga, "De Groots Jodenreglement," in *Mededelingen der Koninklijke Nederlandse Akademie van Wetenschappen*, Afd. Letterkunde 13 (Amsterdam, 1950): 1–8.

10. See *Geschichte des Jüdischen Volkes*, ed. H. H. Ben-Sasson, vol. 3: *Vom 17. Jahrhundert bis zur Gegenwart. Die Neuzeit* (München, 1980), 44f.; 47f.

11. H. R. Trevor-Roper has suggested a later, structurally parallel phase, in his thought-provoking efforts at clarifying the relationship between Calvinism and the Enlightenment: "We find that each of those Calvinist societies [sixteenth-century Heidelberg, seventeenth-century Holland, Puritan England, Huguenot France, eighteenth-century Switzerland and Scotland] made its contribution to the Enlightenment at a precise moment in its history, and that this moment was the moment when it repudiated ideological orthodoxy." "The Religious Origins of the Enlightenment," in *Religion, the Reformation and Social Change and other Essays* (London, 1967), 193–236; 205.

Appendix

Ein wunderbarlich geschichte—1510—

Ein wunderbarlich geschichte. Wye dye Merckischen Juden das hochwirdig Sacrament gekaufft und zu martern sich understanden. Anno domini. 1510.*

Zu wissen, das dysz leufftigen der myndern Zal Im Zehenden Jar: Am Mitwochen nach unnser lieben Frawen Liechtmesz, umb Aylffstundt in der nacht, hat ein böser Christ, mit namen Paul From, der geburt ein Pomer, zu Pernaw gesessen, ein Kesselpüsser, ein morder gewest, ausz teufflischer eingebunge Jn einem dorff knoblach genant, dem bischoff von Brandenburg zugehörig Jn der kyrchen das Cibarium auffgebrochen, darausz ein ubergult puchszleyn, darin zwo consecrirt Hostien, ein grosz unn ein kleyn gewest, sambt einer kupffren vergulten Monstrantzen, gestoln.

Als er aber des volgenden tags umb Achte, nit weyt von dem dorffe Stacka, komen, hat er sich auff einen steyn nydergesetzt, den diebstal besichtigt, und die grossen hostien unwirdigklich vernutzt. Zu handt ist es vinster umb Jne worden. Also, das er lenger dann in einer halben stunndt, nit hat mögen auffstehen, oder weg komen.

Darnach ist er geyn Spandaw (ein Stat, Zwo meyl von Perlyn nach Brandenburg gelegen, do dye haffel und Sprewr zusamen fliessen) gangen, und einem Juden mit namen Salomon die Monstrantzen zu verkauffen angeboten. Darauff Salomon geantwort: wo das gewest, ist mehr gewest. Also hat der bösz Christ das hochwirdig Sacrament ausz dem püszen gezogen, unn umb Sechzehen groschen geboten. Darauf Salomon funff gelegt, und den kauff umb Newn Merckisch, thüt Sechs Sylber groschen, beschlossen.

Darauff ist der gots verkauffer Jnns landt gen wenden zogen, hat

*Translation and commentary, pp. 97–99.

147

aber nit do bleyben mögen, Sonder ist, ungeacht das er gewarnt was, das gerücht berurts diebstals seiner leichtvertigkeyt uber Jne ging, wider anheym zogen. Aldo dye Monstrantzen ausz seinem hauszs uber die mawr geworffen, Die aber ausz gotlicher fursichtigkeyt an einem bäumen hangen peliben. Do sye der Burgermaister funden, unn auff berürte vermütung den dieb gefengklichen angenomen, welher zuhant one alle marter bekant.

Aber Salomon hat das hochwirdig Sacrament auff ein ecken eins Tisch gelegt, darauff ausz hessigen Judischem angebornem neydt, mehrmals gehawen, gestochen, jedoch nit verwunden mögen, bysz so lang er zu zorn bewegt, under vil andern ungestümen worten gefluecht: ›Bistu der Christen got, So erzeyg dich in tausent teufel namen‹.

Auff der stund hat sich von dem stich der heylig fronleichnam Christi wunderbarlich in drey tayl, Jn massen, jne der priester taylt, getaylt. Also, daz die örter blutverbig gewest. Welhe drey Partickel er in seyner taschen vier wochen getragen.

Dweyl er aber mit Jacob, Juden zu Brandenburg, und Marcus, Juden zu Stendel, vor einem halben Jar abgereth unn verlassen: Welher under Jne, das hochwirdig Sacrament uberkeme, solts den andern zuschicken. Hat er den ein Partickel in einem büchszleyn, mit Semischem leder uberzogen, under seynem petschyr genantem Jacob, mit seinem Sone geyn Brandenburg, gleicherweysz den andern Marcus geyn Stendel zugesant.

Jn den Dritten hat er abermals gehawen und gestochen. Also das etlich blutsztropffen herausz geflossen. Den selben Partikel hat er wollen vernutzen, jns wasser werffen, verprennen, und in mancherlay weysz umbringen. Jst jme aber alles onmöglich gewest. Byszsolang er zu Radt worden, das er Jne in ein taygk, ader matzküchen verwurcket, und zu Jrer Ostern jn einen Packoffen geworffen. Und wiewols do zu mal vinster darin gewest, So het er doch zu hant (lauts seiner aygen bekentnüsz) ein klar hell liecht, unn ob dem prot ein schön kleyn kyndlen eins daumen lang, zwaymal schweben gesehen. Wiewol er auch dysz thünsz hart erschrocken des Christen gefengcknusz gewüst, unn geflohen wer, so ist Jm doch von Spandaw zukomen onmöglich gewest.

Den andern Partickel hat Marcus zu Stendel sambt den seinen, als vil an Jne gewest, gleicherweysz zu martern sich understannden, und geyn Braunschwyg, ader als etlich sagen, geyn Franckfurt an Meyn geschickt.

Also hat auch den Dritten Partickel Jacob zu Brandenburg auff ein Tisch gelegt, darein gestochen und gehawen, das man die blutsztropffen miltigklich auff dem Tisch syhet. Wann er hat Jr nit mögen abwaschen oder vertreyben, Sonder einer Span ausz dem Tisch gehawen, den sambt dcm Partickel geyn Osterbürg pracht, da ein gewaltiger Jud, Mayr genant, seinem Sone Jsaac beygelegt, und das hochwirdig Sacrament in einer Schussel verdeckt, der Preut an das peth getragen, mit dysen worten: ›Sye solt sich pillich frewen und geert achten, do precht er Jr der Christen got‹.

Alda haben die Veynd Christi auff der wirtschafft den selben Partickel abermals gemartert. Und Jsaac, der Preutigam, hat Jm von eren wegen den ersten stich geben. Dyser Partickel soll auch geyn Braunschwig komen seyn, do dan die Juden alle gefangen Sytzen. Sonder das prot, Tisch, darauff die plutsztropfen stehn und span, sindt gen Perlyn pracht, do wunderzeichen gescheen, und das Prot thut sich auff, velt und löst sich melich abe.

Es haben auch die verstockten plynten hundt jn der gefencknüsz bekant, Das sye in kurtzen Jaren Syben Christen kynder, Ayns fur Vierundzweytzig groschen, von seiner aygen mutter, einer pewryn, Ayns umb Drey gulden, Auch ains umb Zehen gulden gekaufft die mit nadeln und messern gestochn, gemartert und getodt, das blut mit pareszöpffeln eingemacht, und zu Jrer notturfft gepraucht.

Derhalb hat der durchleuchtigst hochgeboren Churfurst, Margrave Joachim von Brandenburg etc. am Freytag nach Divisionis apostolorum zu Perlyn, den ubeltethern leib und gut aberkennen. Nemlich den Christen, mit Zangen reyssen und verprennen, der gleichen ein besondern Rost auffrichten. Darauff Acht unddreyssig Juden an halszpender schmiden und zu pulver verprennen lassen.

Welche verstockten Juden (das frembdt zu horen, Wo sollichs nit gesehen) mit lachendem mundt das Urteyl angehört, mit Jrem lobgesang auszgefurt. Und auff dem Rost nit allain gesungen und gelacht, Sonnder auch zum tayl gesprungen, geiugzkt, Die verpunden henndt auffgeworffen, das stroh zu sich geraszpelt in die meuler gesteckt. Und also ungeacht der mercklichen wunderzeichen, mit grosser bestendigkeyt den tod gelyden, den pawvelligen Christen zu sunderm erschrecken.

Uber dye genanten haben sich angezaygter Jacob und noch Zwen tauffen lassen. Jacob, Jörg genant, und der ein sein nach volgenndts tags enthaubt, als Christen gestorben; der drit, ein augen artzt, Darumb das er allain an kyndern schuldig gewest, Jst erpeten jns Graw kloster gangen.

Es Sytzen auch noch zu Perlyn bysz Sechzigk Juden, tragen aber von dysem thun keyn wissen. Jst die sag, man werd sye, wie pillich, des lands abermals verweysen.

Getruckt zu Nuremberg durch Hieronymum Höltzel.

INDEXES
by David J. Wartluft

Index of Persons

Index of Places

Index of Subjects

Citation Index:
Authors/Editors

Index of Citations to the
Weimar Edition of Luther's Works